Prai...

"This wonderful c... ...ge of readers… Bill Mellberg has captured the spirit of aviation with this wonderful source book… A great reference for those who love airliners, both past and present." *Jon Proctor, Editor-in-chief,* **Airliners** *magazine*

"William Mellberg has compiled a concise and useful reference on the world's most significant commercial aircraft. Fact-filled and well illustrated, this book provides an informative and entertaining look at commercial aviation." *Brian Baum, Public Information Officer,* **Museum of Flight**, *Seattle*

"Clear and detailed representation of airliners from yesteryear through today. A must for aviation buffs!" *Grace Lucardi,* **American Airlines C.R. Smith Museum**

"Provides many fascinating details of some of the greatest airliners in the history of air travel…amply illustrated. *Famous Airliners* is well written, reads well, and makes a great reference for any airliner aficionado." *Jacquelyn Lanpher, Editor,* **The Atlantic Flyer**

"From noisy, corrugated aluminum fuselages to composites and fly-by-wire, *Famous Airliners* recounts an amazing technological journey." *John Sotham,* **Air & Space/Smithsonian** *magazine*

"William Mellberg displays an enthusiasm for the history of air travel…extensively researched and photographed." *Valerie Vreeland, Review Editor,* **Independent Publisher** *magazine*

"One of the most informative books that we have seen. Attention to detail makes this book a must for anyone interested in aviation." *Charles Lambrou,* **Wings Aviation**

"If you are an airliner or airline buff, this book truly belongs in your library…it is well worth the retail price." *Walt Bohl,* **American Aviation Historical Society** *newsletter*

"Travelers today may complain about the peanuts—or lack thereof—but this comprehensive volume reminds us of a time, not too long ago, when bumpy rides and air sickness were the norm." *Caroline Scutt,* **Travel Weekly**

"A great book for amateurs who are new to aviation or airliners, as well as for experts who have known the field for years." *Sandy Scherner,* **The Pilot Shop**

Famous Airliners

From biplane to jetliner
the story of travel by air

William F. Mellberg

© 1999 William F. Mellberg

ISBN 1-882663-13-6

Plymouth Press, Ltd.

101 Panton Road

Vergennes, VT 05491

On the Web: www.plymouthpress.com

Copyediting by Jan Jones

Plymouth Press has extensive experience in formulating special editions of our books for educational or promotional purposes. Regular and special editions of this book are available at a significant discount when purchased in bulk quantities. To discuss options or for a free quote, call our marketing manager at (800) 350-1007.

Printed in Korea.

Front cover photo: Aérospatiale/British Aerospace Concorde courtesy of British Aircraft Corporation

Back cover photos: Boeing 314 courtesy of Boeing Aircraft; Airbus A300-600ST courtesy of Airbus Industrie.

Dedicated to
Those who dream…and change the world.

Contents

Section Three
The Modern Age of Airliners (1958–present) 112

Introduction

On December 17, 1903, two brothers from Ohio tested an astounding new invention at Kitty Hawk, North Carolina. Orville and Wilbur Wright had designed and built the world's first "aeroplane," succeeding where so many others had failed. Their historic flight was initially questioned by some—and ridiculed by others. Yet, within a few short years, they were demonstrating their "Flyer" to awestruck spectators across America and throughout Europe.

Most people thought of the new flying machine in military terms, envisioning airplanes which could be used to scout enemy positions and to drop bombs on enemy targets. The Wright brothers saw the military potential of their invention—their first sale was to the Signal Corps of the United States War Department. But they also foresaw many civil applications. In 1909, Orville Wright shared his vision in a magazine article. "I firmly believe in the future of the aeroplane for commerce, to carry mail, to carry passengers, perhaps express," he wrote. "We stand at the beginning of a new era—the Age of Flight—and the beginnings of today will be mightily overshadowed by the complete successes of tomorrow."

At the time, few people took the "Age of Flight" very seriously. After all, the early airplanes were no match for trains and ocean liners as a practical means of transportation. Their wooden frames and cloth-covered wings were held together with struts and wires—hardly the sort of machines one could trust to carry people and cargo across vast distances. But on May 20, 1927, a young pilot, Charles Lindbergh, took off from New York and flew nonstop to Paris in a single-engine monoplane he had named the "Spirit of St. Louis." His epic, 33-hour flight captured the world's imagination and demonstrated the growing reliability of aircraft engines and equipment. It also cut the travel time across the Atlantic from four days to a day and a half, a feat that did not escape the attention of visionaries such as Donald Douglas, Anthony Fokker, and Juan Trippe—the men who would design the first airliners and organize the first airlines. Like Lindbergh, they foresaw a time when giant airliners would swiftly carry passengers across oceans and continents on daily flights. Lindbergh's pioneering trip was a technology demonstration which confirmed that view, and inspired an entire generation of engineers and entrepreneurs who then went on to build that future.

Less than half a century after the first powered flight, the "Age of Flight" had become a reality. And with the arrival of the "Jet Age," ocean liners and passenger trains quickly relinquished their dominance of long-distance transport. The world was growing ever smaller. **Famous Airliners** details the evolution of the airliner from rickety fragile biplane to the streamlined supersonic jetliner. But it is also about the men and women who created a magical new form of transportation—and the triumph of the human spirit and imagination over time and distance.

Foreword to the first edition

I first met aviation writer Bill Mellberg in 1987 when he interviewed me for Airliners magazine. He had come to Toronto to talk about the Avro Canada C102 "Jetliner" — the first airplane design for which the "buck stopped" on my desk. I was flattered by Bill's keen interest in the Jetliner, and I appreciated his understanding of its place in aviation history. The Jetliner has too often been forgotten in past works, and I am delighted that Bill has included it in this volume.

Bill Mellberg's insight reflects his extensive experience in the commercial aviation industry. He was a marketing and public relations representative for the Dutch manufacturer, Fokker Aircraft, and has worked for Ozark Air Lines in a similar capacity. He is now a contributing editor for *Airliners* magazine. Bill's byline has appeared in other aviation publications such as *Air Enthusiast*, *Aviation Heritage*, and *Exxon Air World*. He has over 100 published articles to his credit, so he is well versed in aviation history.

I like this book not only because it describes airliners, but because it relates the development of commercial aviation in a way that appeals to casual readers and enthusiasts alike. Although non-technical, it accurately records the technological advances that have taken us from the Wright Brothers' first flight to Neil Armstrong's first step on the moon in less than seven decades.

This rapid progression is of special interest to me since I personally witnessed much of it. And I have known many of the people who made it happen. When I started working for Avro in England in 1930, the company was still building fabric-covered biplanes. Twenty years later, we were flying North America's first jet transport. And less than ten years after that, we were laying the groundwork for the Concorde. **Famous Airliners** describes this remarkable chain of events as well as the people who made such rapid advance possible. While we marvel at the beautiful airliners that take to the sky, we must not forget the men and women behind the scenes who designed, tested, and built these technological wonders. I know how hard they worked to bring their dreams to reality.

I am therefore pleased to write this foreword and to recommend **Famous Airliners**. It is a wonderful collection of photographs and essays. As you read it, I hope you will be reminded of something I tell my friends and colleagues in the aviation industry: "If it seems to be impossible, then do it anyway… because it's usually the very difficult or almost impossible things that are most worthwhile." That is the philosophy that has guided aeronautical engineers from the Wright Flyer to the Space Shuttle. Those words summarize the real message of this book.

James C. Floyd

During his long career in aviation, Jim Floyd worked with some of the world's greatest aircraft designers, including Sir Sydney Camm of Hawkers (producer of the Hurricane and Harrier) and Roy Chadwick of A.V. Roe (Anson and Lancaster). Jim and his wife, Irene, were both involved with the Lancaster bomber at Avro during the war years. In 1946, Jim was appointed Chief Design Engineer at the newly formed A.V. Roe Canada where he led the technical team that produced North America's first jet transport, the C102 Jetliner. As Vice President of Engineering for Avro Canada, he was responsible for the supersonic CF-105 Arrow fighter. Later he returned to England to work on the Concorde and other advanced projects. Among his many honors, Jim Floyd has been awarded the Wright Brothers Medal (1950), the J.D. McCurdy Award (1958), and the Royal Aeronautical Society's George Taylor Gold Medal (1961). He was inducted into Canada's Aviation Hall of Fame in 1993.

Section One
The Pioneering Era (1925–1934)

Lufthansa's Ju 52/3m airliners made regular flights into London Airport at Croydon before the start of World War II. (Airbus Industrie/Hartmut Klein)

In the early days of commercial aviation, flying was a real adventure, and passengers were true pioneers. It took both courage and wealth during the Depression years to be able to board a fabric-covered biplane like the Boeing Model 80 for a 32-hour multi-stop cross-country flight. Air travelers in the 1920s enjoyed few of the amenities taken for granted in modern jetliners. The planes were slow, and at low altitudes, where the air can be rough and the weather severe, they often bounced along. The roar of the engines could be deafening, and the vibration from the propellers rattled bones—and nerves. Airsickness was a common passenger complaint.

Airports and airliners were also very different from what people are accustomed to today. The terminals usually resembled bus depots rather than the great, cathedral-like railway stations of the era. This meant a structure consisting of a waiting room with a ticket counter and a few wooden benches. There might be a cafe where one could grab a hot meal before the flight (cold sandwiches were the usual fare on board). Early airliners suffered from severe payload restrictions—baggage had to be carefully weighed and seats were assigned so that the plane would be balanced while in flight.

Once a flight was announced, passengers would walk down a short sidewalk to their waiting aircraft. There were no jetways, although an awning might provide some protection from the elements. People had to literally climb aboard, as most early airliners were "tail draggers" resting on their tail wheels, rather than being supported on an even level by the tricycle landing gears which are standard on most modern airliners. As a result, the cabin floors were inclined while on the ground, and one had to struggle a bit against gravity in order to reach a forward seat.

When the flight was ready, the pilots would fire up the engines. Each motor sputtered to life, rocking the plane and spewing clouds of blue and white smoke. Bouncing along what was often a grass-covered airfield, the airplane would reach the end of the airstrip, the pilots would advance the throttles, and the rickety machine would head off into the wild blue yonder. The ferocious roar of the engines turned conversations into shouting matches. Many passengers would stuff cotton wads into their ears to reduce the noise; most suffered a temporary hearing loss at the end of each flight.

Still, the advance of technology during the late 1920s and early 1930s made air travel increasingly attractive. Lockheed's streamlined little Vega delivered speed; Ford's sturdy Tri-Motor offered reliability; the Curtiss Condor introduced luxury. And the modern low-wing all-metal designs of the Boeing 247 and Douglas DC-2 heralded the more advanced airliners of the future.

With every new design, airplanes grew bigger, faster, and safer. In these adolescent years of commercial aviation, the foundations were laid for a giant new industry, and the trails were being blazed for a global transportation network.

This beautifully restored Boeing Model 80 can be seen at the Museum of Flight in Seattle, Washington. (Museum of Flight)

Chapter 1
Boeing Model 80

The year was 1927. Calvin Coolidge was President of the United States. Among the most popular songs being played were *Blue Skies* and *Let A Smile Be Your Umbrella*. Sound had just come to the movies with Al Jolson in The Jazz Singer. And Prohibition was giving rise to gangsters such as Bugs Moran and Al Capone. It was the Roaring Twenties.

At the end of that year, a new era in transportation began when the Chicago Municipal Airport (renamed Midway in 1949) was dedicated on a square mile of property southwest of the city's central Loop. Its cinder runways, boundary lights, and revolving beacon (which made night flights possible) represented major innovations. While Europe had been served by several pioneering airlines for nearly a decade, this was the beginning of America's vast transcontinental air transport system, thus making Chicago the birthplace of modern commercial aviation.

The first flights into the new airport carried sacks of mail, not people. Up to this time no one had designed an airplane which could profitably carry only passengers, so the fledgling carriers relied on government mail contracts to survive. Boeing Air Transport (BAT), a division of the Boeing Airplane Company, won the airmail route between Chicago and San Francisco in January 1927 and began service with a fleet of 24 Boeing Model 40A and Model 40B biplanes. These were single-engine machines with open cockpits for the pilot and a small cabin for two passengers (later four) between the mail compartments.

The success of the Model 40 encouraged Boeing to design a much larger biplane tailored to carrying passengers. The Model 80 was first flown on July 27, 1928, and went into service just two weeks later. It was equipped with three engines, cruised at 115 mph, and was flown by two pilots in an enclosed cockpit, itself an innovation at the time. Twelve passengers were accommodated, together with baggage, freight, and mail.

The Model 80 was described as the "Pioneer Pullman of the Air." It was, indeed, a considerable advance over the earlier Model 40. The passenger cabin included such luxuries as forced air ventilation, hot and cold running water, leather upholstered seats, and a lavatory. Four Model 80s were built for BAT's route linking San Francisco and Chicago. Passengers could make connections in Chicago to eastbound flights. By 1929, the coast to coast travel time was reduced to 32 hours, wind and weather permitting. This was a great improvement over train schedules although rail service was still more dependable and less noisy than air transport.

The first of 11 improved Model 80As entered service in 1929. These airplanes had more powerful engines and could carry up to 18 passengers in three-abreast seating, although the usual configuration was for 14 seats. Cruising speed was increased to 125 mph, but the airplane's 14,000-foot service ceiling was barely enough to clear the Rockies. By mid-1930, BAT was making daily roundtrip flights along the Chicago route. Each trip could include a dozen stops along the way.

Another new dimension in air travel began with the Boeing Model 80. Early in 1930, a young nurse named Ellen Church made an intriguing proposal to BAT's management. A flight enthusiast, she wanted to employ other young nurses as "flight attendants." Some of the European airlines were already flying with stewards, but copilots were handing out sandwiches and apples on board BAT flights. Church believed nurses would be better able to care for passengers since flying could still be a somewhat unnerving experience. Though reluctant at first, BAT executives finally agreed to try the idea for three months. Ellen Church became BAT's Chief Stewardess, and she hired seven more nurses from hospitals in San Francisco and Chicago. Each was paid $125 per month for 100 hours of flying. Together, they became the world's first stewardesses.

This Boeing Model 80A was lost in 1943 while flying with Reeve Airways in Alaska, when it was ditched at sea, fortunately without loss of life. It had been delivered on October 1, 1929. (Boeing)

The interior of the Boeing Model 80 featured leather seats and passenger reading lamps. A lavatory was in the rear. The airliner shown here was in service with Boeing Air Transport. (Boeing)

Passenger reaction was overwhelmingly positive. Letters poured into the airline praising the young girls who were creating a new profession. In rough weather, it was both helpful and reassuring to have the flight attendants doing their best to make each passenger comfortable. In addition, air travelers enjoyed the fried chicken, hot soup, and coffee, which had replaced box lunches and thermos jugs.

The Model 80 performed admirably during its short service life. One former pilot called it "one of the most rugged and safest airplanes Boeing ever built." It had a solid look and inspired confidence in both passengers and crews, even though, other than the nose section, the entire airframe was covered with fabric. Technology continued to advance rapidly, however, and the Model 80 quickly became obsolete. Withdrawn from regular airline service in 1933, it was supplanted by another Boeing design, the sleek all-metal Model 247, which would make its own mark on aviation history. But the old trimotors flew on a while longer with secondhand operators. One specially built Model 80A served as an executive plane for Standard Oil Company. Boeing got out of the airline business in 1934, but the BAT subsidiary became the nucleus of today's giant United Airlines. Meanwhile, the Seattle-based company eventually became the world's leading manufacturer of commercial airliners. Likewise, Chicago soon established itself as the world's busiest air transportation hub.

Only one example of the Boeing Model 80 still exists, a beautifully restored machine on display at Seattle's Museum of Flight. It serves as a splendid reminder of a bygone era—and the beginning of a giant industry. While the Model 80 was not the best known airliner ever built, it was certainly one of the most important. And, in addition to its other firsts, the Model 80 was noteworthy as the first purpose-built airliner to bear the famous Boeing name.

Chapter 2
Fokker F. VII-3m

The world's most successful airliner during the late 1920s and early 1930s was the Dutch-designed Fokker F.VII-3m. While many people associate the name Fokker with World War I and Germany's Manfred von Richthofen (the "Red Baron"), the firm originated in Holland, where it still provides support for its airliners today. In fact, Fokker's reputation over the years was built more on its trimotor transports than its triwing fighters. And many of the most famous flights of that period were flown with an airplane that became the standard for air travelers around the globe — the Fokker Trimotor. It pioneered today's air routes.

The son of a coffee plantation owner, Anthony H.G. Fokker was born on April 6, 1890, in Blitar, a tiny settlement on Java in the Dutch East Indies. When Tony was four years old, his parents decided to return to Holland so that he and his older sister could obtain a proper education. In Haarlem he was known as a mischievous but inventive youth, qualities which remained with him for the rest of his life.

In 1931, Fokker published a controversial autobiography. Although he was only 41 years old, his name was already known around the world for his aviation achievements. The book was appropriately titled *The Flying Dutchman*. In his introduction to the book,

Fokker's first F.VIIa-3m at a stop during the 1925 Ford Reliability Tour. (Fokker)

Eddie Rickenbacker (the American fighter ace and later president of Eastern Air Lines) wrote about his first encounter with Fokker airplanes. This had occurred during World War I when he met an enemy Fokker D-VII in the skies over France. Rickenbacker believed the Allies had made a great mistake in failing to enlist the talents and services of the Flying Dutchman, and he praised the Fokker transports that Eastern Air Lines was operating at the time of the book's publication. In just over a decade, Rickenbacker's career had taken him from shooting at Fokkers over France to flying them over America.

Fokker began his autobiography by describing how he had designed and flown his own airplane as a young man in 1910. He had first heard about airplanes as a 23 year-old boy, and from that day on he was determined to become an aviator. He fulfilled that dream in 1911, demonstrating his tiny *Spin* (Spider) in the skies over Haarlem to admiring crowds below.

Traveling to Germany in 1912, young Fokker established Fokker Aviation Limited and tried to sell a more advanced version of the Spin to various customers. He peddled his machine without success in Russia, England, Italy, and Holland. Finally, his designs were taken up by the Germans in 1913. Not long after that, German airmen were gaining victories with Fokker fighters over the Western Front. Fokker also invented the synchronized machine gun which turned his airplanes into the "Fokker Scourge."

The Flying Dutchman—Anthony Fokker. (Fokker)

Charles Kingsford-Smith was the first man to fly across the Pacific Ocean in his Southern Cross, *a Fokker F.VII-3m Trimotor. A replica of that famous aircraft is shown here.* (Fokker)

In 1922, two US Army air pilots, O.G. Kelly and J.A. Macready, flying a Fokker T–2, became the first men to fly nonstop across America. In 1926, Commander Richard E. Byrd and Floyd Bennett made the first flight over the North Pole in Henry Ford's Fokker Trimotor, *Josephine Ford,* named after Edsel Ford's youngest daughter. The following year, Byrd flew another Fokker from New York to Paris just a few weeks after Lindbergh's trip. Amelia Earhart became the first woman to cross the Atlantic in 1928 using a Fokker, and in the same year, Australian aviator Charles Kingsford-Smith became the first to cross the Pacific in his *Southern Cross,* another Fokker.

The Trimotor itself was more properly known as the Fokker F.VII-3m. It was a three-motor (thus, "3m") variant of the highly successful single-engine F.VIIa transport, which was already in use on long-distance routes. After the war, Fokker had returned to Holland where he started building airliners, beginning with the F.II. The F.VII series was a highly-evolved version of the earlier model.

In 1924, Fokker established a US subsidiary, and during a visit to America the next year, he learned that Henry Ford was organizing a competition to stimulate public interest in commercial aviation. Fokker decided to enter the 1925 Ford Reliability Tour with a three-engine version of his F.VII. The airplane was emblazoned with the Fokker name, resulting in the press's dubbing the tour the "Fokker Reliability Tour." Fokker was first at every stop, winning the Ford Trophy handily in his ten-passenger airliner.

After the tour, Fokker offered his Trimotor to the world's airlines, and they purchased it in large numbers. Over 200 Fokkers, following the basic F.VII-3m design, were built and sold, making the type Fokker's most successful airliner before World War II. England's Avro Aircraft produced the plane under license as the Avro Ten, and the Trimotor was built in the United States as the 12-passenger F.10 and the slightly larger F.10A. The popular Trimotors featured mahogany interiors and padded wicker seats. But when the legendary football coach, Knute Rockne, was killed in the crash of a TWA F.10 in 1931, Fokker's fortunes in America rapidly faded, and the wooden winged airplanes were withdrawn from service. Fokker continued to manufacture trimotors in Holland up until 1932 with the F.XVIII model.

Anthony Fokker died prematurely in a New York hospital on December 23, 1939, the victim of an infection following a nose operation. His remains were returned to Holland where he was buried in the family vault near Haarlem. A stone bird mounted on a pedestal marks the site, commemorating his career and his many contributions to aviation.

Today, Fokker airliners still ply the world's air routes. But sagging sales and rising costs forced the company to file for bankruptcy in early 1996. Its last newly built airliner emerged from the firm's sprawling Schiphol works near Amsterdam in 1997, although Fokker will continue to support its existing products. While another famous manufacturer has now disappeared, its airliners will proudly carry the Fokker name for many years to come.

Chapter 3
Ford Tri-Motor

In recent years, twin-engine jetliners have dominated airline fleets. Starting with short-haul transports in the 1960s, the twin-engine configuration has been increasingly adopted for larger and longer-range airliners, a trend made possible by the ever increasing power and reliability of modern jet engines. This strategy also contributes to airline economics since two engines are generally less costly to maintain than three or four.

But during the 1920s, when airplane engines were not so reliable, three motors were considered necessary for safety's sake by both airlines and manufacturers. Thus, trimotor transports were the accepted norm. Trimotor designs were produced in England, Holland, Italy, Germany, the Soviet Union, and the United States. But of all the three-engine transports, the Ford Tri-Motor, affectionately dubbed the "Tin Goose," was the best known. Its fame and popularity had more to do with its durability and widespread use than with the Ford name and logo which were proudly displayed on its tail.

This Ford Tri-Motor 5-AT stands in front of an American Airways hangar circa 1930. (American Airlines)

What Henry Ford had done for the automotive industry with his Model T Tin Lizzie, he attempted to repeat for the aviation industry with his Model 4-AT and 5-AT Tin Geese. His goal was to make modern transportation—on either wheels or wings—available to the average citizen. Ford had not invented the automobile, but his introduction of the assembly line enabled mass production of inexpensive cars, changing American society and culture. In a similar manner, he helped to give birth to many of today's airlines though he produced fewer than 200 of his Tri-Motors between 1926 and 1932. While he did not invent the modern airliner, the Tin Goose was a critical step in its development.

The Ford Tri-Motor was noteworthy on two counts: its all-metal construction and its three-engine layout. Neither was in itself unique. In 1919, the Junkers firm in Germany had produced an all-metal airliner with a corrugated duralumin skin. Ford chose a new alloy called Alclad that combined the corrosion resistance of aluminum with the strength of duralumin. The engine configuration was copied directly from the Fokker F.VII-3m Trimotor.

Henry Ford's interest in aviation stemmed, in part, from the efforts of his 23 year-old son, Edsel, to build an airplane in 1909. The younger Ford worked with several of his friends and succeeded in producing an airplane that did fly—barely. A few years later, during World War I, the Ford Motor Company produced the famous Liberty engines for

This Ford Tri-Motor, restored to its original appearance, is now on display at the National Air and Space Museum in Washington, D.C. (American Airlines)

This beautifully restored Ford Tri-Motor was flown at the Experimental Airplane Association's Fly-in at Oshkosh, Wisconsin, in 1990. Eastern Air Transport eventually evolved into Eastern Air Lines, which went out of business in 1991. (Bill Mellberg)

American-built de Havilland warplanes. By 1925, Henry Ford was building his own civil transports through his ownership of the Stout Metal Airplane Company.

William B. Stout was both an engineer and a promoter. He believed that airplanes would never advance very far using wood and fabric for their construction. Hearing about what Junkers was doing in Germany, Stout designed and built his own all-metal machine called "The Bat," which first flew in 1920. The US Navy showed some interest in the plane but never made a purchase, so Stout turned to the civilian market.

The following year he wrote a letter to Edsel Ford who by that time was running the Ford Motor Company. Stout offered an unusual proposal. "I should like a thousand dollars, and I can only promise you one thing," he wrote. "You'll never see the money again!" In response, Ford sent him a personal check for $1,000 plus another $1,000 from his father. Stout had other famous sponsors as well, but his relationship with the automobile manufacturer got him a factory to build his airplanes in 1924.

The design he produced carried the Ford logo and was dubbed the 2-AT (for "Air Transport"). It was a single-engine machine with which Ford established his own cargo airline to carry parts and priority shipments between his plants in Dearborn, Cleveland, and Chicago. That operation was so successful that Ford asked Stout to create a larger, trimotor airplane. The resulting Model 3-AT was an ungainly craft that was destroyed in a hangar fire shortly after its first flight. The blueprints burned in the blaze as well.

When Anthony Fokker won the 1925 Ford Reliability Tour with his F.VII-3m Trimotor, Ford bought the airplane for Commander Richard E. Byrd's historic flight over the North Pole in 1926. Ford then turned his trimotor project over to several young engineers, including Harold Hicks, Thomas Towle, and James McDonnell (who later founded the McDonnell Aircraft Corporation). Late one night during a clandestine "measuring party," the new team measured every inch of Byrd's Fokker. When the new Ford 4-AT design was revealed, it bore an amazing resemblance to Fokker's Trimotor!

The new Ford Tri-Motor first took to the air on June 11, 1926. During the next seven years Ford produced 198 of his Tri-Motors, including the slightly larger and more advanced Model 5-AT. Airlines around the world placed Fords into service, and a few of the old Tri-Motors were still flying 60 years later. In some countries, the Ford name was synonymous with airplanes rather than automobiles!

The Tin Goose was a safe, rugged, and reliable machine. However, few passengers called it comfortable. A flight in a Ford was slow, noisy, and bumpy. Its 12 wicker seats (14 in the 5-AT) were not equipped with safety belts, and the cabins were usually either too hot or too cold. Airsickness was a common affliction, but the large windows and high wing provided excellent views of the ground passing below.

Over 100 airlines and cargo operators eventually flew Ford Tri-Motors. Commander Byrd used a ski-equipped version to fly over the South Pole in 1929. Franklin Roosevelt flew a Tri-Motor from Albany to Chicago to accept the Democratic Party's presidential nomination in 1932. Like the Fokker it had been based on, the Ford Tri-Motor recorded many firsts and nurtured many fledgling airlines. Although Henry Ford left the airliner business in 1933, his Tin Goose will live forever in the annals of aviation history.

Chapter 4
Junkers Ju 52/3m

While the overall design of the Ford Tri-Motor might have been "borrowed" from the Fokker F.VII-3m, its corrugated skin was copied from the sturdy Junkers transports that were being built at the time in Germany. In fact, when the four-passenger Junkers F 13 made its maiden flight on June 25, 1919, it also made history as the world's first all-metal airliner. Between 1919 and 1932, over 300 of these little one-engine monoplanes were produced, contributing to the development of air transportation around the globe. But for our story, the real significance of the F 13 is that it led directly to the development of another famous trimotor—the legendary Junkers Ju 52/3m.

Dr. Hugo Junkers was born in Prussia on February 3, 1859. A brilliant young man, he studied thermodynamics and later became a professor of physics at the Technical High School in Aachen. Junkers was also an entrepreneur and inventor, founding his own company, Junkers Werke A.G., at Dessau in 1895. The firm produced gas furnaces

The Junkers' corrugated skin and trailing edge "double wing" can be seen in this view of Lufthansa's restored Ju 52/3m. (C.F.A.P. collection)

A Lufthansa Ju 52/3m rests on a rain-soaked tarmac in this scene typical of European airports in the mid-1930s. (Lufthansa/Hartmut Klein)

and hot water heaters. By 1910, the Professor had taken an interest in aeronautics and obtained a patent for an aircraft wing design which was years ahead of its time. Not surprisingly, he also worked on new ideas for his own aircraft engines.

In 1915, Junkers produced his first airplane, called the "'J 1." The precursor of the F 13 airliner, it was the first all-metal aircraft ever built. Like nearly all of Junkers' subsequent designs, the F 13 used steel tube frames covered by corrugated aluminum skin. This was truly an innovative approach at a time when wooden frames were still being covered with fabric and held together with struts and wires. Starting with the F 13, Junkers' metal transports earned a worldwide reputation for their rugged reliability and safety. In fact, in 1921 the Professor established his own airline, which later became part of Lufthansa German Airlines.

Having enjoyed success with the F 13, Junkers refined the basic design building the W 33 and W 34 in 1926. These were generally similar to their famous predecessor, although they were a bit larger, seating up to six passengers. The W 34 had a radial engine instead of the in-line types used on the F 13 and W 33. In 1928, a W 33 named *Bremen* became the first airplane to fly nonstop across the North Atlantic from east to west. The publicity generated by that flight helped Junkers' sales across the globe, with aircraft going to such diverse regions as the Canadian bush country and the jungles of South America. Junkers also produced two trimotor transports in this period called the G 23 and G 24 which were essentially scaled-up versions of the F 13, carrying as many as nine passengers. The company built a huge, four-engine airliner called the G 38 in 1929, two of which would serve with Lufthansa. The 34-seat G 38 featured a very large wing; six passengers actually sat in its leading edge where they enjoyed a spectacular view!

Junkers aircraft were known for their ability to haul cargo, and the single-engine Ju 52 was built specifically as a freighter. The prototype took off from Dessau on October 13, 1930. It could carry a 2-ton payload nearly 1,000 miles, and its unobstructed cabin and large door facilitated loading of bulky items. Only a handful of Ju 52s were produced, the last one going to Canadian Airways where it was known as the "Flying Box-car" and was used to carry everything from mining equipment to livestock. The Ju 52 had the same corrugated aluminum skin used on other Junkers aircraft, plus a

The Junkers Ju 52/3m transport was a familiar sight in many parts of the world during the 1930s. (C.F.A.P. collection)

patented "double wing" system consisting of full-length flaps and ailerons which improved airfield performance and allowed short runway takeoffs and landings.

One early Ju 52 was fitted with three Pratt & Whitney Hornet engines built under license by BMW. This version was called the Ju 52/3m (the "3m" standing for three motors). First flown in April 1932, this particular model of the Ju 52 would go on to earn both fame and notoriety—for while hundreds of examples of these aircraft entered service as airliners, thousands more flew in military roles with Adolf Hitler's Luftwaffe. This fact, no doubt, would have displeased Hugo Junkers, whose opposition to the Nazi regime sent him into involuntary retirement in 1934. He died the following year on his 76th birthday.

Junkers did live to see the Ju 52/3m become the dominant European-designed airliner of the 1930s. Its economical operation and sturdy construction resulted in sales in over 30 different countries. Germany's Lufthansa had the largest fleet, consisting of 78 of the trimotors at the advent of World War II. Others saw service in Europe, Africa, Asia, South America, and North America.

The Ju 52/3m carried 14 to 17 passengers, plus a crew of two pilots and a flight attendant. Seats were on either side of a center aisle with a lavatory and baggage hold at the rear of the cabin. Lufthansa pilots hoisted a small company flag above the cockpit while the airplane was on the ground, and many of the carrier's Ju 52s were named for World War I German airmen (e.g., *Manfred von Richthofen*). One of Lufthansa's trimotors was used as Hitler's personal transport, appearing in the opening sequences of Leni Riefenstahl's infamous propaganda film, *Triumph of the Will*. (Many years later, another Ju 52 was used in the title scenes of the film, *Battle of Britain*.)

The civil Ju 52s were soon overshadowed by the military models, with a bomber version appearing in 1935. It equipped the first Luftwaffe bomber squadrons and was used to support Franco's forces during the Spanish Civil War. The Ju 52, in full production throughout World War II, served primarily as a troop transport and freighter, becoming more affectionately known as "Tante Ju" ("Auntie Ju") and "Iron Annie." Some 5,000 Ju 52 trimotors were built, including several hundred assembled in France and Spain. The Spanish Air Force flew the type until 1975.

At least two of the Junkers are still flying, including a beautifully-restored model in Lufthansa colors which has been seen at a number of airshows in recent years. Although its appearance is most reminiscent of the Ford Tri-Motor, Hugo Junkers' Ju 52/3m earned a reputation for service, adaptability, and longevity that was second only to the immortal Douglas DC-3.

Chapter 5
Lockheed Vega

Two streamlined and elegant airplanes grace the galleries of the Smithsonian Air and Space Museum in Washington, D.C. Both are Lockheed Vegas. One is the blue and white Winnie Mae in which Wiley Post made the first solo around-the-world flight in 1933 as well as several other record-breaking trips. The other, painted bright red, was the airplane in which Amelia Earhart became the first woman to fly solo across the Atlantic Ocean and then the United States in 1932. Like many other famous pilots of their day, Post and Earhart had a great deal of faith in the Vega.

Today the Vega is best remembered for its speed and record-shattering flights. But it was designed as an airliner, and it was as an airliner that the Vega laid the foundation for Lockheed's future success. The Lockheed name originated from the family name (Loughead) of the three brothers who founded the company. Because the Irish spelling was usually mispronounced "Log-head," they changed it to "Lockheed" (the phonetic spelling) in 1921.

In 1910, when he was 20 years old, the youngest brother, Allan, traveled to Chicago to join Victor, the oldest brother. Allan was interested in both airplanes and automobiles, and both Victor and Malcolm, the middle brother, were automotive engineers. Allan

A restored Lockheed Vega displays the airplane's clean lines. The Vega was famous for its speed, which was made possible by its streamlined shape and enclosed engine. (Lockheed)

took a job as a mechanic for Victor's boss, James E. Plew, who was the Chicago distributor for White steam cars and Curtiss airplanes. He was also president of the Aero Club of Illinois. Victor was a club officer along with Harold McCormick, the son of Cyrus McCormick, who had invented the mechanical reaper and was the founder of the giant International Harvester Corporation. Victor Loughead and Harold McCormick organized Chicago's first international air show in 1911.

Allan Loughead learned to fly in Chicago using Plew's Curtiss Pusher. But he soon returned to California where he and Malcolm designed and built a small seaplane in 1913. Its success encouraged the brothers to hire a self-taught engineer, John Northrop, to help them with their next design. Northrop, just 21 years old at the time, would eventually be recognized as one of the most brilliant aeronautical engineers of all time. He helped Allan design a capable seaplane, dubbed the F-l, which they hoped to sell to the US Navy. However, despite its excellent performance, the Navy ordered Curtiss seaplanes.

The Lougheads and Northrop pressed on with another design for the sport market. The S-l was a streamlined airplane which pioneered many innovations in design and construction. It was years ahead of its time in 1919. But because of the glut of surplus warplanes on the civilian market, not a single S-l was sold. As a result, Loughead Aircraft was liquidated in 1921. Malcolm moved to Detroit where he became rich and famous for his invention of the hydraulic brake system which is still used in automobiles. Allan sold real estate, and Jack Northrop went to work for Donald Douglas.

In 1926, Allan Lockheed and Jack Northrop designed an all-plywood monoplane in their spare time. They found a wealthy investor who helped them form a new Lockheed Aircraft Company, and they put all of their energies into creating the most advanced airplane of its time — the Lockheed Vega.

Named for one of the brightest stars in the sky, the Vega was a revolutionary design. Like the S-l, its cigar-shaped fuselage was made of molded plywood, fabricated in two halves and glued together to produce an extremely smooth surface. It was suspended from an equally clean wing which helped give the Vega its superior speed. The Vega made its first flight from a field in Los Angeles on July 4, 1927. Coming less than two months after Lindbergh's flight to Paris, the four-passenger Vega created a sensation with its top speed of over 150 mph.

The graceful Vega gained quick recognition when the third airplane built was used for a series of Arctic flights by Sir Hubert Wilkins in 1928. Lockheed built 64 Vegas at its Burbank plant that year. Sales increased when the Vega won all of the speed trophies at the 1928 National Air Races in Cleveland. The company's slogan became, "It takes a Lockheed to beat a Lockheed!"

Northrop left Lockheed in June 1928 and was replaced by Gerald F. Vultee (who would also leave in 1930 to form his own company). As the Vega came into widespread airline use across the country and around the world, the basic design was improved and

To maximize speed this Lockheed Vega was equipped with wheel pants, also known as "fairings," which streamlined the landing gear and reduced resistance. This model is similar to Wiley Post's famous Winnie Mae, *which is on display at the National Air and Space Museum in Washington, D.C.* (Lockheed)

modified. The speed and power of the Vega were increased, as was the seating capacity (to six). In addition, the parasol-winged Air Express and low-wing Orion with retractable landing gear were sold to both foreign and domestic airlines during the next few years. The Orion was an especially trim-looking airplane which could reach a top speed in excess of 200 mph, considerably faster than most of its contemporaries.

Passengers appreciated the speed offered by Lockheed's "plywood bullets." But with so few seats, the Vega and its offshoots could not be regarded as practical airliners. The major advantage they offered was speed, and busy executives were more than willing to pay premium fares to get it. In that sense, the Vega demonstrated the need for a high-speed high-capacity airliner. While Lockheed was producing the Orion, Boeing was flying its Monomail, an experimental low-wing design that laid the foundation for the next major advance in air transport.

Meanwhile, Lockheed was having its share of financial problems. The company had been sold to the Detroit Aircraft Corporation in 1929, and that firm filed for bankruptcy in 1931. The following year, a group headed by Robert E. Gross bought Lockheed's

The low-winged Orion shown here was an advanced design based on the Vega. The new model featured retractable landing gear to maximize speed. (Lockheed)

assets for a mere $40,000. Many new and exciting chapters were then added to the firm's history. Lockheed continued to produce airplanes built for speed, such as the famous P-38 Lightning and SR-71 Blackbird. Each wore the same Winged Star insignia that had been created for the fabulous Vega. Allan Lockheed stayed with the company as a consultant until his death in 1969. The company he had given his name to, had by that time, become an industrial giant. In 1995 it merged with another company with a famous name and a long tradition to form the Lockheed Martin Corporation.

Chapter 6
Curtiss Condor

The Wright brothers might have invented the airplane, but Glenn H. Curtiss was responsible for giving America its wings. More than any other individual during the pioneer years of flight, he advanced the cause of aviation in general and of the American aircraft industry in particular. Unfortunately, the Wrights and Curtiss did not work together during the early years—the two brothers initiated a protracted legal battle against Curtiss, accusing him of infringing on their patents. Ironically, the Curtiss Aeroplane and Motor Company was merged with the Wright Aeronautical Corporation in 1929 to form the Curtiss-Wright Corporation. By that time, the surviving Wright brother, Orville, and Glenn Curtiss had relinquished control of their respective firms, and had settled their past differences.

Glenn Curtiss was born on May 21, 1878, at Hammondsport in western New York. Like the Wrights, he started his own bicycle business. But unlike the Ohio brothers, Curtiss liked to race cycles, leading him to design a small engine to power his bikes. This natural combination became a great success, and Curtiss motorcycles were soon being sold all across the country. Curtiss himself set a record in 1907, racing a motorcycle at over 136 mph.

Dr. Alexander Graham Bell heard about the Curtiss motorcycle engines and in 1907 he invited the young designer to his summer home at Baddeck, Nova Scotia. Dr. Bell had been interested in the possibilities of flight for many years, and at the suggestion of his wife (and with her financial support), formed the "Aerial Experiment Association" (A.E.A.) that October. In addition to Bell, the members included Curtiss; two young Canadian engineers, Casey Baldwin and John A.D. McCurdy; and Lieutenant Thomas Selfridge of the US Army (who, the following year, became the first person to die in an airplane crash while flying with Orville Wright at Ft. Myer, Virginia).

The A.E.A. set about designing and building several airplane designs. The work—as well as initial flight testing—was done at the Curtiss plant in Hammondsport. Their first airplane, the *Red Wing*, was ready in March 1908. It flew—briefly, proving the basic design and paving the way for incremental improvement. Next came the *White Wing*, followed by the *June Bug,* which won the Scientific American Trophy on July 4, 1908 by making the world's first one-kilometer flight. The fourth machine, dubbed the *Silver Dart*, made the first flight in Canada the following February. In March 1909, the *Silver Dart* flew more than 20 miles. All of the A.E.A. aircraft were powered by Curtiss engines.

The A.E.A. was disbanded in 1909 when Curtiss entered into a short-lived partnership with Augustus Herring. In 1911, he formed the Curtiss Motor Company (which, in turn, controlled the Curtiss Aeroplane Company). His airplanes and airplane engines were soon setting one record after another. Glenn Curtiss produced the first flying boats, as well as the famous JN-4 Jenny military trainers and their OX-5 engines during World War I. After the war, Curtiss aircraft and powerplants continued to lead the way in aviation development. In 1919, the Curtiss NC-4 flying boat completed (in stages) the first trans-Atlantic flight. Sadly, Glenn Curtiss died, prematurely, on July 23, 1930, the victim of appendicitis. He was 52 years old.

The Curtiss-Wright Corporation lived on. While most of the firm's airplanes were produced for the military, the Curtiss B-20 Condor was an 18-passenger transport derived from an earlier bomber design. Only six of them were built, all going to Eastern Air Transport. The first of the twin-engine biplanes took to the air on July 21, 1929. Their careers were quite short, remaining in service with Eastern for just a few years before being put up for sale.

A completely new "Condor" appeared in 1933. Designed during 1932 under the leadership of George A. Page, Jr., the Curtiss-Wright T-32 Condor was built at the

Passengers are seen boarding the first production model Curtiss-Wright T-32 Condor, delivered to American Airlines in April 1933. (American Airlines)

The AT-32 version of the Condor entered service in 1934. American Airlines flew 19 Condors, including ten AT-32s. (American Airlines)

company's St. Louis plant and made its maiden flight on January 30, 1933, just nine days before the far more revolutionary Boeing 247. This Condor was a highly-refined, twin-engine biplane with a semi-retractable landing gear and a roomy cabin that carried 15 passengers by day. It was far more comfortable than its trimotor contemporaries, and at night the seats could be converted into a dozen Pullman-style sleeping berths. With its powerful Wright Cyclone engines and advanced cockpit instrumentation, the Condor was designed to compete with the railways on long-distance overnight trips.

Eastern Air Transport and American Airways each ordered five of the new Condors. The first deliveries were made in the spring of 1933, with Eastern sending them out on its New York to Miami route, and American flying them coast to coast. The Condors looked particularly resplendent in American's colors with their dark blue fuselages and bright orange stripes and wings. Additional orders were placed by both airlines, with American eventually flying 19 Condors including ten of the improved AT-32 models. Passengers appreciated the Condor's modern amenities — as well as its emphasis on cabin soundproofing.

Curtiss-Wright also sold several military versions of the airplane, and Admiral Richard E. Byrd used one during his second Antarctic expedition in 1933. Other Condors went to customers in Europe, Asia, and Latin America. Production ended in 1934 after a total of 45 aircraft had been built.

Despite the model's popularity, it was no match for the Boeing 247 and Douglas DC-2 which followed it into service. A mere three years after its introduction, the Condor was no longer flown by either Eastern or American, although a few soldiered on into the 1950s with secondhand operators. The Condor was the last biplane transport produced in the United States, and as such, its career was bound to be short-lived. However, as we shall see, its success as an overnight sleeper did lead to the development of the legendary Douglas DC-3.

Chapter 7
Boeing Model 247

When the Chicago World's Fair, dubbed the "Century of Progress," opened in May 1933, one of the star attractions was the brand new Boeing Model 247 airliner. Despite the gloom of the Great Depression, both the Fair and the airplane offered a vision of a brighter future.

For the Model 247, the future was only a few weeks away. It went into service in June, and was greeted enthusiastically all across the nation. Crowds lined the fences at airports to see the planes, and those lucky passengers who boarded the silvery 247s knew they were flying in a revolutionary new airliner. When the 247 made its maiden flight from Boeing Field in Seattle on February 8, 1933, one of the company's engineers proclaimed, "They'll never build 'em any bigger!"

Thirty-six years later, on February 9, 1969, that same engineer might have eaten his words during the first flight of the Boeing 747 — an airplane which was more than 50 times as heavy and almost five times as long as the 247, and which could carry 50 times as many passengers! But no matter how great the differences might be, all of today's modern airliners can trace their roots to the 247.

The first Boeing Model 247 during a typical boarding operation. (Boeing)

The ten passengers aboard the Boeing 247 each enjoyed a large window and a plush seat. However, passengers seated in the rear had to step over the wing spar, visible just in front of the flight attendant. (Boeing)

The Boeing 247 introduced the concept of the all-metal low-wing multi-engine airliner. Its streamlined shape, smooth skin and semi-retractable landing gear were all very advanced features compared to other passenger transports of the time. Most historians regard the 247 as the first truly modern airliner. Cruising at 189 mph, it reduced the coast to coast travel time to 19½ hours (flying at over three miles a minute).

The aerodynamic foundations of the 247 were in the Boeing Monomail airliner first flown in 1930 and in the Boeing B-9 bomber which flew a year later. The Monomail was an all-metal low-wing adaptation of Boeing's Model 40 biplanes. It was built to fly over the same routes on Boeing Air Transport's passenger and air mail system. Although it was never placed into production, two prototype Monomails were put into service on BAT routes and successfully demonstrated many of the design features later used in the 247. The Monomail eventually evolved into the twin-engine B-9 and had a great influence on the design of the Model 247. All were products of the Boeing Airplane Company, which had been founded in 1916.

William E. Boeing was born in Detroit, Michigan, on October 1, 1881. The son of a prosperous lumber merchant, Boeing graduated from Yale University in 1904 and soon established his own successful lumber business in Seattle. Bill Boeing had a reputation for thoroughness. It surprised no one who knew him when, after his first seaplane ride in 1914, he decided he could build a better machine.

One of Boeing's friends was a United States Navy officer, Commander Conrad Westervelt. The two men designed the Type B&W floatplane in 1915. By the time it made its first flight the following June, Westervelt had been transferred to the East Coast. The B&W flew well, and several examples were sold by Boeing's Pacific Aero Products Company. On April 26, 1917, the firm adopted a new name — the Boeing Airplane Company. It was destined to become the world's leading manufacturer of commercial jetliners.

The Boeing 247 was the first truly modern airliner, and marked the end of the "strut and wire" era.
(Boeing)

Boeing got into the commercial aviation business in 1926, when he created the airline division of the Boeing Airplane and Transportation Corporation. Three years later, he joined several other aviation-oriented companies to form the United Aircraft and Transportation Corporation (UATC). Among the members were such famous names as Sikorsky, Pratt & Whitney, and Hamilton-Standard, together with several smaller airlines which were reorganized as United Air Lines in 1931.

Early the next year, United ordered 59 Model 247s while the airplane was still in the development stage. This unprecedented move was designed to replace the fleets of the four airlines which flew under United's umbrella. The ten-seat Model 247 opened a new era in air transportation when it was delivered the following summer. The airplane represented a tremendous advance over the Boeing and Ford trimotors that Boeing Air Transport had been flying even though it had a smaller cabin. Unfortunately, the 247's instant success also proved to be its downfall.

When TWA tried to buy some 247s for its own routes, the directors of the United Aircraft conglomerate informed the airline that it would have to wait until United's 59 airplanes had been delivered. This forced TWA to turn to another manufacturer, Douglas Aircraft. The result was the DC-2, which entered service in 1934. Just a year after its own spectacular arrival, the 247 was destined to become obsolete, although it remained in service with United for the next eight years.

Meanwhile, antitrust laws caught up with United Aircraft. In 1934, the US government broke UATC into three separate companies—United Aircraft Corporation, United Air Lines, and the Boeing Aircraft Company. Never again would a single corporation be allowed to manufacture its own airplanes, engines, and propellers in addition to flying its own routes.

Bill Boeing withdrew from active participation in the company in 1933. The next year, he received the Guggenheim Medal "for successful pioneering in aircraft manufacture and air transportation." He turned his attention to fishing and cattle breeding for the next 20 years. But before his death in 1956, he saw the roll-out of the 707 prototype —the first of the famous Boeing jetliners.

As for the 247s, they flew on with a number of secondhand operators well into the 1960s. Various improvements had been introduced over the years, and United used one of its 247s as a flying research laboratory. Scientists were able to study weather-related problems as well as static which interfered with air-to-ground radio communications. Another United-owned 247 placed third in the MacRobertson Air Race from England to Australia in 1934.

Altogether, Boeing sold 75 of its 247s. The airlines, however, needed an even better airplane—one that could carry more people in greater comfort at less cost. The Boeing 247's technology lead would prove to be short lived.

Chapter 8
Douglas DC-1 and DC-2

The years between the stock market crash of 1929 and the beginning of World War II in 1939 were marked by some stark contrasts. It was the decade of the Great Depression — a worldwide economic calamity that gave rise to political and social upheavals. It was also an era of great advances in technology. In particular, nationwide radio broadcasts and popular motion pictures were bringing people together in new and exciting ways. The depression could be forgotten for a few hours while watching Laurel and Hardy's antics at the cinema, or listening to Will Rogers on the radio. Politicians also recognized the growing influence of mass communications. In the United States, Franklin Roosevelt used the airwaves to overcome fear. In Germany, Adolf Hitler used technology to create it. And the rapid development of science was giving rise to advances in many other fields — including warfare.

"Science, which offers us a golden age with one hand," warned Winston Churchill, "offers at the same time with the other, the doom of all that we have built up inch by inch since the Stone Age and the dawn of human annals." In speaking of the wonders of

An American Airlines DC-2 at Chicago Municipal Airport — later renamed Midway — in the mid-1930s. A Ford Tri-Motor can be seen in the left background. (American Airlines)

modern technology, he added, "Let us make sure that they are our servants, not our masters."

Aviation generated the most enthusiasm during this era, and the airplane was increasingly regarded as a servant of mankind. Its ability to offer high-speed travel between distant places resulted in its recognition as an alternative form of communication. Entire continents could now be crossed in less than a day, but given the economic reality of the period, air travel had to become more cost-effective. The lumbering biplanes and trimotors already in airline service depended on government subsidies to break even. What was needed was a fast, modern airliner that could make money carrying passengers alone. In 1932, Transcontinental & Western Air, Inc. (TWA), called upon the aircraft industry to produce just such an airplane. The call was answered by the Douglas Aircraft Company in Santa Monica, California.

A vintage photo of a DC-2 interior during a typical flight. Note that meal service included china, metal eating utensils, and glass salt and pepper shakers. Flying has indeed come a long way since these times! (Douglas Aircraft)

The New Douglas 14-Passenger Airliner

SALON 26' LONG x 5'6" WIDE
x 6'3" HIGH SEATS 40" APART
GIVING GENEROUS ACCOM-
MODATIONS FOR 14 PASSEN-
GERS.

DIRECTIONAL BEAM
RADIO ANTENNA.

RETRACTABLE RADIO
ANTENNA.

FULL HEAD ROOM.
UNOBSTRUCTED AISLE.

COLD AIR VENTI-
LATING DUCT.

STEAM HEATING
SYSTEM.

SALON IS COMPLETELY SOUND-
PROOFED AGAINST ALL NOISE
AND VIBRATION, MAKING IT
QUIETER THAN A PULLMAN.

LAVATORY AND
AUXILIARY ENTRY
TO BAGGAGE.

2-WAY VOICE RADIO MAIN-
TAINS CONTACT BETWEEN
GROUND AND PLANE ALSO
FOR WEATHER AND DIREC-
TIONAL BEAM SIGNALS

EXCLUSIVE ALL-METAL
MULTI-CELLULAR STRUC-
TURE PRODUCES GREATEST
KNOWN STRENGTH-WEIGHT
RATIO.

DOUGLAS
AIR BRAKES
REDUCE
LANDING
SPEED TO
MINIMUM.

112 CU. FT. BAGGAGE AND
CARGO COMPARTMENT.

TWIN 700 H. P. ENGINES AND
CONTROLLABLE PITCH THREE-
BLADE METAL PROPELLERS
GIVE A SPEED OF 210 M.P.H.
AT 8000 FT.

ICED BUFFET AND SERVICE CABINET.

SPACIOUS PILOT'S COM-
PARTMENT WITH COM-
PLETE DAY AND NIGHT
FLYING, ENGINE AND
NAVIGATION INSTRU-
MENTS. DUAL CONTROLS

COMPLETE STREAMLINING. NOTE
METHOD OF "FLOWING" ONE SUR-
FACE INTO ANOTHER, CONTRIBU-
TING TO HIGH SPEED PERFORMANCE.

VENTILATION INTAKE
IN NOSE AHEAD OF
ENGINES CONTRIBUTES
TO CABIN QUIETNESS

DOOR TO 76 CU. FT. MAIL
COMPARTMENT.

LANDING LIGHTS.

WHEELS RETRACT INTO
ENGINE NACELLES.

INDIVIDUAL READING LIGHT,
ASH TRAY, SERVICE BUTTON,
APPAREL RACK AND VENTILA-
TION CONTROL.

LOUNGE CHAIRS 24" WIDE WITH REMOVABLE HEAD
RESTS MAY BE FULLY RECLINED OR REVERSED. INDI-
VIDUAL WINDOWS AFFORD EXCELLENT VIEW

A 1933 promotional figure for the DC-2 championed the many new features of the revolutionary airliner.
(Douglas Aircraft)

Donald W. Douglas, Sr., a brilliant engineer and shrewd businessman, was born in New York on April 6, 1892. His father loved the sea and wanted the boy to join the Navy. But when he was 17 years old, Douglas saw Orville Wright demonstrating an early Wright Flyer to the United States Army Signal Corps at Fort Myer, Virginia. Although Douglas entered the US Naval Academy a few months later, his dreams turned to the sky. After three years at Annapolis, the young man transferred to the Massachusetts Institute of Technology, earning a degree in aeronautical engineering in 1914. He stayed on at MIT as a research engineer, and then worked as the chief engineer for the US Army Signal Corps before joining the Glenn L. Martin Company, one of America's pioneer aircraft manufacturers. In 1920, Donald Douglas moved to California where he started his own business.

Jack Frye, TWA's Vice President of Operations, had tried to purchase the Boeing 247. But Boeing's 247 production run was already committed to its sister company, assets for $40,000. His partners included aircraft designer Lloyd Stearman and airline president Walter Varney. They continued to produce Lockheed's "plywood bullets." But with the advent of Boeing's Model 247 and of the Douglas DC-2, it was clear that a new airplane was needed for Lockheed to remain competitive in the air transport business.

Lloyd Stearman and a young aeronautical engineer named Hall Hibbard began work on a new all-metal twin-engine design. This would become Lockheed's Model 10. In keeping with the company's tradition of dubbing its airplanes after stars, Electra, one of the Seven Sisters in the Pleiades star cluster, was chosen as the name for the new transport. It was destined to become the cornerstone of the new Lockheed Aircraft Corporation.

The Electra was originally designed with a single fin and rudder, but wind tunnel tests at the University of Michigan at Ann Arbor showed that the airplane might suffer control problems in the event of an engine loss. The young engineer who made this discovery was Clarence "Kelly" Johnson. He recommended a twin-tail design, and soon both Johnson and his ideas had migrated to Lockheed's Burbank factory in California.

A brand new Lockheed Model 10 Electra on the tarmac at the company's Burbank plant. Amelia Earhart flew a similar plane in her ill-fated attempt to circumnavigate the globe. (Lockheed)

A Lockheed Model 14 Super Electra in Northwest Airways colors. This scaled-up Electra served as the basis for the famous Hudson bomber in World War II. (Lockheed)

Johnson was later to play a primary role in the design of such famous Lockheed airplanes as the P-38 Lightning, the supersonic F-104 Starfighter, and the triplesonic SR-71 Blackbird. He was one of the world's greatest aeronautical engineers and remained a fixture at Lockheed long past his retirement in 1975.

With this nucleus of talent and ideas, Lockheed proceeded quickly with the development of the Electra. The airplane's first flight took place on February 23, 1934. Like its contemporaries, the Electra featured sleek lines and a semi-retractable landing gear. Indeed, apart from its twin-tail, Lockheed's Model 10 reminded passengers of a somewhat smaller Boeing 247.

The ten-passenger Electra entered service with Northwest Airlines between Minneapolis and Chicago on August 11, 1934. The type soon became a familiar sight at countless airports. The Electra was an even bigger success than the Vega and, like its predecessor, was the fastest airliner in the skies. In 1937, Amelia Earhart flew an Electra on her ill-fated attempt to become the first woman to fly around the globe. But the airplane was best known for its service with airlines such as Pan American, Trans-Canada, KLM, and British Airways. Altogether, 149 Electras were built.

To complement the Electra, Lockheed developed a smaller six-passenger version called the Model 12 Electra Junior. First flown in June 1936, this airplane was used primarily as an executive transport and military machine, although it had been designed with feeder-line commuter services in mind.

A more significant development was the Model 14 Super Electra, which was a scaled-up version of the Electra. It could carry 12 passengers, together with a crew of three (including a flight attendant). Its maiden flight took place on July 29, 1937, and 112 examples were sold to such major airlines as Northwest, Continental, British Airways, KLM, Trans-Canada, and Sabena. Northwest, which put the airplane into service in October of that year, dubbed its Model 14s "Sky Zephyrs," a play on the famous high-speed railway Zephyrs of that era.

The Super Electra featured a number of innovations such as Fowler flaps, which were pioneered by Lockheed. These flaps shortened takeoff runs and landing rolls, and they earned Kelly Johnson the 1937 Lawrence Sperry Award. While the Super Electra retained the same layout as the Model 10, it was a much larger airplane with a more spacious cabin.

The Super Electra was chosen by multimillionaire aviator Howard Hughes for his record-breaking, around-the-world trip in July 1938. The four-day flight earned Hughes the Harmon Trophy, the Collier Trophy, the Chanute Award, hundreds of other awards and citations, a Congressional Medal, and a huge ticker tape parade through New York City. Hughes said at the time, "If credit is due anyone, it is due to the men who designed and perfected to its remarkable state of efficiency the modern American flying machine and equipment."

Just two months later, another Super Electra, this one flown by British Airways, carried British Prime Minister Neville Chamberlain, back to London from his infamous Munich Conference with Adolf Hitler. Standing beside the Lockheed airliner, Chamberlain waved the Peace Declaration he had signed with the German dictator. The following September, Britain was at war, and the Royal Air Force was flying a militarized version of the Model 14, called the Hudson. Thousands of RAF Hudsons served throughout the war in a variety of roles from light bombers and utility transports to air ambulances.

Meanwhile, Lockheed flew its 14-passenger Model 18 Lodestar (a stretched Model 14) on September 21, 1939. But by that time, the company's attention, like the world's, was focused on more immediate concerns, and Kelly Johnson was facing even more important design challenges.

Section Two

Air Travel Comes of Age (1935–1957)

Tying up the Boeing 314 flying boat at a mooring was an experience which emphasized the extent to which the airliner really was a "boat." (Boeing)

Up until the mid-1930s, traveling by air was a luxury for the rich or a novelty for the adventurous. Unfortunately, it was also a money-losing proposition for the airlines. While early airliner models laid a foundation for the future of the air transport industry, they were unable to contribute black ink to the bottom line. Indeed, airlines needed government subsidies and mail contracts just to break even. But the strides made in aviation technology during this economically depressed period were soon to make passenger air travel a practical possibility for everyday folks—and profits a reality for the airlines. One aircraft in particular symbolized this change: the Douglas DC-3.

With the advent of the DC-3, commercial aviation finally established itself as a legitimate alternative to railways and steamship lines. The DC-3 was large enough to carry enough passengers far enough and economically enough to create a revolution in travel. Moreover, the DC-3 inspired a whole new breed of advanced airliners. For example, in 1938, Boeing incorporated a pressurized cabin and four turbo-supercharged engines in its cigar-shaped Stratoliner. At the same time, Lockheed was working on a similar, though larger, transport called the Constellation. And Douglas was touting its own tripled-tailed giant, the DC-4E. The trend was swiftly being established for bigger, faster, and safer airliners.

There were some interesting sidebars during this period. Flying boats, such as the fabled "Clippers" produced by Martin and Boeing for Pan American Airways, helped to establish air routes across the world's great oceans. Vying for the transatlantic market, Germany's huge dirigibles—*Graf Zeppelin* and *Hindenburg*—offered unrivaled luxury in the air, and halved the travel time of the fastest steamships. The tragic explosion of the Hindenburg at Lakehurst in 1937, however, ended the airship era. But the flying boats soldiered on throughout the war years.

World War II accelerated the advance of new technologies, bringing about major innovations in aircraft structures and powerplants. Less than five years after the war, the first jetliners were flown and propeller-driven behemoths, such as Boeing's glamorous Stratocruiser, were competing with ships and trains on long-distance routes. Moreover, short-haul transports, including secondhand DC-3s, were bringing airline service to many smaller communities for the first time. By the mid-1950s, air travel had come of age.

Chapter 10
Douglas DC-3

The immortal Douglas DC-3 has been the recipient of more plaudits, the subject of more fond tributes, and the hero of more true-life stories than any other airplane in history. Originally known as the DST (Douglas Sleeper Transport), the elegant DC-3 became the most famous airliner ever to grace the airways — and for good reason. During its long career the DC-3 was the backbone of many of the world's air carriers. It was built in larger numbers than any other aircraft in its class and it flew to every corner of the globe. It served with distinction during World War II, in Korea and Vietnam, as well as in dozens of other conflicts. It played an important role in the Berlin Airlift.

In this view of the interior of an American Airlines DST, taken shortly after the model entered service, a pilot shows a passenger the flight path. The airliner's seats converted into beds at night. Note the overhead berth in its folded position above the pilot's head. (American Airlines)

An American Airlines' DC-3 "Flagship" flies above the clouds in this early color photograph. Note the semi-retractable main landing gear. (American Airlines)

Along the way, it picked up many nicknames: "Sky Sleeper," "Gooney Bird," "Dakota," "Sky Trooper," "Sky Train," and "Puff the Magic Dragon" — to name just a few.

But despite its tremendous success, the DC-3 almost never happened. When C.R. Smith, the dynamic and visionary young president of American Airlines, approached Douglas in 1934 about building a Pullman-style sleeper version of the DC-2, the manufacturer was hesitant. After all, the company was already busy turning out the profitable DC-2. Douglas was also concerned that the market for a sleeper transport was limited and that its development costs would eat into the DC-2's profits.

But American Airlines desperately needed a more modern aircraft to replace its fleet of Curtiss Condor biplanes and Ford Tri-Motors. Smith saw the answer in a sleeper version of the 14-seat DC-2 designed to serve American's transcontinental routes. So he persisted, offering to buy 20 aircraft from Douglas, which was equivalent to the TWA order that had launched the DC-2. Douglas accepted, and Jack Northrop and William Littlewood, American Airlines' chief engineer, created what would become the DC-3.

In order to accommodate 14 sleeping berths on long overnight flights, the DC-2's fuselage was lengthened by some 2½ feet and made two feet wider. The wings were extended, the fin and rudder were enlarged, and more powerful engines were installed. The takeoff weight went up by 7,000 pounds although the cruising speed came down slightly to 185 mph.

The first flight of the DST took place on December 17, 1935, and delivery to American Airlines was made on June 8, 1936. C.R. Smith met the airplane in Chicago after its nonstop flight from California. Service between Chicago and New York started shortly thereafter, and coast to coast flights were inaugurated that September.

The DST created quite a sensation, and American played up the new airplane for all it was worth. Each DST was named after a city or state (e.g., "Flagship California"), and together they were dubbed the "Flagship Fleet." Smith knew about publicity. He had his copilots hoist a flag bearing the company's eagle insignia above the starboard cockpit window as soon as each flight landed. It would be waving proudly as the DST rolled up to the gate while newsmen shot pictures of the deplaning celebrity passengers. And when child star Shirley Temple sang "On The Good Ship Lollipop" for the cameras, she was supposedly aboard an American DST.

After World War II, many DC-3s were sold to the new "local service" airlines. This DC-3 was used by Trans World Airlines. (Airliners America)

The airplane attracted the rich and famous as well as business executives who preferred the 16-hour overnight flight to a much longer cross-country train trip. A private compartment known as the Sky Room was available for VIPs willing to pay an extra fare. All passengers were treated to sleeping berths comparable to those offered by the railroads but with a far more impressive view. Flight attendants pampered them with complimentary cocktails and juicy steaks. The pilots on these "Mercury" flights would come back to the cabin to talk with the passengers. In the morning, dressing rooms were provided to freshen up after a night of "sleeping on air." This was a new era in air travel.

The success of the DST flights was such that American—and many other airlines— soon decided to use the airplane on shorter, daytime routes. The 14-passenger DST now became the 21-passenger DC-3. Douglas could barely keep up with the orders. By 1938, the DC-3 was carrying a staggering 95 percent of all airline traffic in the United States, and before World War II brought a halt to most civil air operations, 90 percent of the world's airline traffic was being flown by DC-3s! The type was also produced under license in Japan and the Soviet Union (as the Lisunov Li-2).

During World War II, more than 10,000 military DC-3s were built. These were designated C-47s and R4Ds by American forces, and Dakotas by British services. They were used to carry cargo, personnel, and supplies. On D-Day, more than a thousand C-47s darkened the skies over Normandy, dropping paratroopers and towing troop-carrying gliders for the invasion.

After the war, most of the DC-3s and many of the C-47s returned to civilian duties. Although initially placed on mainline routes, they were soon sold off to regional carriers, bringing regular air transportation to many smaller communities for the first time. Others flew in developing countries in more remote parts of the world.

Today, hundreds of DC-3s and C-47s are still carrying freight and passengers and still earning money for their owners. More than 50 years after the DST first entered service, the world's oldest DC-3 was put up for sale. It had already flown 91,380 hours, the equivalent of flying nonstop for over ten years. In that time it had traveled more than 13 million miles, the equivalent of nearly 30 roundtrips to the moon. It had worn out countless spark plugs, engines, and tires—not to mention carrying countless passengers.

Yet the airplane was not dispatched to a museum. Rather, an advertisement stated that it was "in immaculate condition and still in current service." Most experts believe that some DC-3s will still be flying when the airplane celebrates its 75th birthday in 2010, and a few might even be around for its 100th. That, perhaps, is the greatest tribute to arguably the greatest airliner of all time—the DC-3!

Chapter 11
Douglas DC-4E

During the summer of 1939, Adolf Hitler and his Wehrmacht generals were planning the invasion of Poland — the trigger that would set off history's most devastating conflict. But on the other side of the Atlantic, most Americans had more pleasant thoughts on their minds. Prosperity, at long last, really did seem to be just around the corner. Joe DiMaggio was hitting home runs for the Yankees. *Gone With the Wind* was the talk of Hollywood and visitors to the New York World's Fair could see visions of a more promising future. And at airports across the country, the shape of things to come had already arrived in the form of a giant new airliner called the Douglas DC-4E.

The DC-4E was a one-of-a-kind experimental airplane (thus, the "E" designation) that United Air Lines was evaluating on its routes. The four-engine triple-tailed craft was one of the biggest most luxurious and most technically advanced transports of its time.

The Douglas DC-4E at Santa Monica Airport after its maiden flight. Of interest are the triple rudder and the second row of narrow windows for the upper berths in the sleeper configuration.
(Douglas Aircraft)

It came about as a result of a joint undertaking between Douglas Aircraft and the airline industry to build upon the success of the DC-2 and DC-3. In fact, the DC-4E was being planned even before the DC-3 had made its first flight.

The impact of the DC-2 on air transportation was enormous, and some airline executives already envisioned bigger and better airplanes that could carry more people more quickly and over greater distances. Foremost among these dreamers was United Air Lines' new president, William A. Patterson. The carrier had just become a separate entity from Boeing, so "Pat" was free to discuss his dream plane with all of the major manufacturers. Only Donald Douglas took a serious interest in the project although he expressed the opinion that the cost of developing such a bold new airliner would be too much for his company to underwrite alone. Patterson offered to pay for half of it. Douglas, in turn, suggested that United join forces with several other airlines to come up with a common list of requirements for the "Superliner."

Five domestic carriers — United, American, Eastern, TWA, and Pan American — pooled their ideas and agreed to a set of specifications. They also agreed to pool their money, and in March 1936, they each committed $100,000 toward the design and construction of a DC-4E prototype. Douglas was responsible for the remainder of the development costs.

The resulting airplane had a wing which resembled the DC-3's but was 43 feet longer. The fuselage was similar as well, but was both longer and fatter. The distinctive, low-profile triple-tail was chosen in order to fit the DC-4E into existing airline hangars. The big transport also featured a number of innovations, such as a fully-retractable tricycle landing gear, an auxiliary power unit which could generate electrical power while the airplane was on the ground, air conditioning in the cabin, and flush-riveted skin. Less obvious features incorporated the latest advances in materials, structures, and aerodynamics.

The cabin was designed to seat 42 passengers by day and 32 by night. The first truly modern galley provided fine cuisine. A men's lounge and a ladies' lounge were each outfitted with a lavatory and a full-length divan. Pullman-style sleeping berths were provided for long distance night flights, and a "honeymoon suite" had its own lavatory and washroom. The plush seats in the main cabin could be made up as beds or reversed to form groups of four for daytime socializing.

The DC-4E took off on its maiden flight on the afternoon of June 7, 1938. Some 30,000 spectators were at Santa Monica Airport to witness the event, and the flight made headlines around the world. During the next few months, a number of problems arose with the DC-4E's new and complex systems. But they were ironed out one by one, and on May 4, 1939, the airplane was given its Approved Type Certificate — clearing the way for airline evaluation and demonstration flights.

Veteran pilot Benny Howard put the DC-4E, repainted in United Air Lines colors, through its paces on United's routes from coast to coast. Along the way, hundreds of

An interior view of the Douglas DC-4E showing how the seats converted into double beds. The upper berth folded into the ceiling during the day. Curtains provided privacy at night. This arrangement was similar to railway Pullman cars. (Douglas Aircraft)

thousands of people came out to local airports to see the giant. A lucky few even got to walk through the new plane. All were impressed by its size and ultramodern interior.

Unfortunately, the airlines were not so impressed. Two members of the original quintet, TWA and Pan American, had already dropped out of the project, having decided to order Boeing's smaller and less complex Stratoliner. By the time it was airborne, American and Eastern had concluded that the DC-4E was too big to be practical and too costly to maintain. The airplane never flew their routes. Even United's engineers had their doubts, reflected in a long list of improvements they suggested that would have increased the cost of an airplane which had already become far more expensive than originally estimated.

United returned the airplane to Douglas, and the DC-4E was abandoned in favor of a smaller less sophisticated unpressurized design. This single-tailed DC-4 would also carry 42 passengers, and it was ordered by United, American, and Eastern. But by the time the new DC-4 took to the air in 1942, the United States was deeply involved in World War II. Hundreds of militarized C-54s were produced and used as troop and cargo transports. One C-54, dubbed *Sacred Cow,* was specially modified to serve as a VIP aircraft for President Franklin Roosevelt. After the war, surplus C-54s and newly-built DC-4 airliners finally went into commercial service with air carriers around the globe.

The DC-4E prototype was sold to Japan before the war in the fall of 1939. The airplane disappeared shortly after its arrival in Tokyo. It has been suggested that the DC-4E was disassembled and studied in some detail. The Nakajima Shinzan bomber, after all, had a nearly identical wing as well as some of the same problems as the DC-4E.

Douglas lost well over one million dollars on the DC-4E, but the airplane paved the way for the highly successful postwar DC-4, DC-6, and DC-7 series. In 1939, the visionary DC-4E truly did represent the shape of things to come.

A few DC-4s, which came after the DC-4E, are still in use. Here, a postwar single-tailed DC-4, smaller than the DC-4E, is seen plying the airways of Air North, a Canadian airline. (Air North)

Chapter 12
Martin 130 and Boeing 314

There was never more romance associated with an airliner than with Pan American Airways' famous Clippers. Actually, the name, "Clipper," was applied to many different types of Pan Am aircraft, starting with its Sikorsky S-40 flying boats in 1930. But two types, in particular, are remembered as the quintessential Pan Am "Clipper" ships — the Martin 130 and Boeing 314 flying boats. These magnificent airplanes were known for their luxurious appointments and their exotic destinations. They spanned oceans, not continents. They flew to Honolulu, Manila, Fiji, and Hong Kong. Along the way, passengers enjoyed full-course meals served on linen-covered dining tables with fine chinaware. Travelers could relax in a comfortable lounge during the day and recline in private sleeping compartments at night. Pan Am's Clippers offered the ultimate in First Class travel during the 1930s.

Pan Am studied, and then adopted, many maritime practices to the operation of its flying boats. The captain of each Clipper was known as a "Master of Ocean Flying

The Pan Am Martin 130 China Clipper *in flight over California. Pan Am's Clippers pioneered trans-Pacific flights.* (Pan American Airlines)

Boats," since the captain of a ship was often called a master. Pan Am called copilots "First Officers;" navigators, "Second Officers;" and engineers, "Third Officers." Kitchens were called galleys. While on the water — as opposed to in the air — the crews, who were required to be familiar with port, starboard, red lights, green lights, buoys, flag codes, and other nautical terms and procedures, observed a protocol very similar to that of the merchant marine. They had to become basic seamen in order to become airmen. Before each flight the crew marched in double file to the flying boat with the captain in the lead, an impressive sight with the men decked out in Pan Am's navy blue uniforms and white caps.

But why a flying *boat*? What was the purpose of mating a hull with wings? The answer to these questions starts with the founding of Pan American Airways by a young aviation pioneer named Juan Trippe. A Yale graduate and naval aviator, Trippe won a contract in 1927 to fly the mail between Key West, Florida, and Havana, Cuba. The service began that October, using a single-engine Fairchild FC-2 equipped with floats. The Fairchild was a substitute for Pan American's Fokker F-7 land plane because the runway at Key West's Meacham Field had not been completed. During the next few years, Pan Am expanded its route system throughout Latin America. At many of its stops, the airline had to construct its own facilities, hacking runways out of jungles, setting up weather stations, and building hotels and hangars to house passengers, crews, and airplanes.

Pan Am's Caribbean network formed a great circle, and it included numerous islands and coastal cities. For these routes, the airline decided to use Sikorsky S-38 amphibians. The Sikorsky carried the same number of passengers as the Fokker, but it eliminated the need for expensive runways where water landings could be made. Furthermore, at a time when commercial aviation was still in its infancy, it reassured travelers to know that their plane could touch down in the sea if any trouble developed. For this reason, flying boats were being built by aircraft manufacturers around the world.

Charles A. Lindbergh, who in 1927 flew the *Spirit of St. Louis* from New York to Paris, joined Pan Am as a technical advisor in 1929. His job was to evaluate new aircraft and new services for the company. He shared Trippe's vision of air routes circling the globe. By 1935, Pan Am was ready to take on the biggest challenge of all — air service across the vast Pacific. The airline turned to the Glenn L. Martin Company to produce three giant, four-engine flying boats. These Martin 130s were dubbed "Pacific Clippers," but they were better known as "China Clippers" after the first plane to be delivered and after a movie of the same name. The *China Clipper* initiated air service to Manila on November 22, 1935. Carrying up to 46 passengers in a very plush cabin, the Clipper made four stops along the way: Honolulu, Midway Island, Wake Island and Guam. The San Francisco to Honolulu leg was the longest, at just over 2,400 miles. The entire trip to the Philippines covered 8,200 miles, and the route was soon extended to Hong Kong. It took six days to cross the Pacific aboard Pan Am's Clippers, including overnight stops

The Boeing 314 Clippers were the ultimate flying boats. Pan Am used them to inaugurate trans-Atlantic air service, as well as to replace the China Clippers in the Pacific. The crew flew the plane from a flight deck above the passenger cabin. (Pan American Airlines)

along the way. By comparison, a trip to the Orient by steamship took three weeks!

The success of the trans-Pacific service created the need for an even larger flying boat. In 1936, Pan Am signed a contract with Boeing to build six (later 12) new B-314s. These four-engine behemoths were designed to cross both the Atlantic and the Pacific. The first B-314 was delivered in 1939. At the time, it was one of the largest airplanes ever built—and certainly one of the most luxurious. The crew sat upstairs on the flight deck while up to 70 passengers enjoyed spacious accommodations in the cabin below. Like the Martin Clippers, the Boeing Clippers were divided into individual compartments. Off-duty officers, including the captain, would join passengers in the dining salon for dinner. Movie stars and the rich and famous often traveled in Clippers, a fact which explains their glamorous reputations.

Flying the Clippers was not without its inconveniences. The 17-hour trip between California and Hawaii did take its toll on one's hearing—the drone of the big propellers hour after hour could be deafening. With only crude instruments for navigation and communication, it was something of a miracle that the Clippers found their way to tiny islands in the middle of a seemingly endless ocean. Pan Am crews and passengers were genuine pioneers in transoceanic air travel, and at the time, most people thought of a trip aboard one of the flying boats as a grand adventure.

The Clippers were drafted into military service during World War II. After the war, long-range land planes replaced them on the world's air routes. But Pan Am's Clippers had already blazed the trail for the postwar era's transoceanic travelers.

The dining cabin of a Boeing 314. Note the spacious structure with high ceilings. This level of comfort explained how the M-130 and B314 flying boats became symbols of luxury and service (Boeing)

Chapter 13
LZ 129 *Hindenburg*

Flying boat passengers were not the first to cross the oceans by air. Thousands of travelers had already flown from continent to continent in the largest, most luxurious "airliners" ever built — Germany's giant, rigid airships (also known as dirigibles or Zeppelins). These aerial behemoths were as big as most ocean liners, and offered a similar standard of luxury. The last of the breed to see scheduled service was the majestic LZ 129 *Hindenburg*. Its fiery demise in 1937 marked the end of the airship era—and the passing of a marvelous mode of travel. But, for a time, it looked like the future belonged to Zeppelins.

The Hindenburg *over New York City as it heads toward a landing at the Naval Air Station at Lakehurst, New Jersey. The giant airship was as big as an ocean liner, but crossed the North Atlantic in half the time.* (John Mellberg collection)

Travel aboard the Hindenburg *was luxurious, as can be seen in this view of the airship's 50-foot long dining room, where stewards served gourmet meals prepared by the cook and five assistants. To the left of the dining room is the port promenade deck where passengers could enjoy the view through panoramic windows.* (John Mellberg collection)

Three years before the Wright Brothers' first flight, Count Ferdinand von Zeppelin had invented a new kind of balloon. Actually, his "airship" consisted of a series of 17 balloons inside a cloth-covered cigar-shaped metal framework. The "balloons" were, in fact, gas bags filled with hydrogen. Since hydrogen gas is lighter than air, the combined volume of the gas bags was enough to lift the weight of the vehicle. Two 12 hp engines drove four propellers which gave the ship its forward speed, and rudders and elevators controlled its direction. The first of the new rigid airships was called the LZ 1 for "Luftschiff Zeppelin 1" (Airship Zeppelin 1). It took off from a floating hangar on Lake Constance ("Bodensee" in German) on July 2, 1900. The flight lasted just 20 minutes, but the 62-year-old Count's dream had become a reality.

Unfortunately, the LZ 1 was severely underpowered, which made it impractical. After three flights, von Zeppelin had it dismantled. But he persisted, and five years later launched his "new and improved" LZ 2. The experimental ship crashed during its first flight!

Finally, with the help of a brilliant engineer, Ludwig Durr, the Count achieved success with his LZ 4 in 1908. It made an impressive 12-hour round-trip to Switzerland.

The 804-foot long Hindenburg's *four engine gondolas (two on each side) and the small control car mounted beneath the nose are clearly visible in this view. The starboard promenade windows can be seen between the Olympic rings and the* Hindenburg's *painted name.* (John Mellberg collection)

But that August, the LZ 4 crashed and burned when it was caught in a storm. The disaster nearly ruined von Zeppelin, who had invested all of his assets in the airship enterprise. However, the LZ 4 had created quite a sensation before it was destroyed, and the Count quickly became an overnight hero in the eyes of his countrymen. They sent him all manner of gifts, including the money to build another "Zeppelin."

With each new airship, new ideas were tested and new lessons were learned. Luftschiffbau Zeppelin GmbH was organized at Friedrichshafen in 1908 to manufacture the dirigibles, and Deutsche Luftschiffahrt Aktien-Gesellschaft (better known as DELAG) was formed the following year to carry passengers. Scheduled service between German cities, however, was not introduced until after World War I. But between 1910 and 1914, some 10,000 passengers enjoyed sightseeing trips over the German countryside, sipping on champagne while safely seated in a lavish cabin built into the bottom of each Zeppelin hull. Flying slowly, a mere few hundred feet above the ground, the views were spectacular.

Ferdinand von Zeppelin died in 1917. During World War I, his firm built over 100 military airships. After the war, the Zeppelin company was taken over by a trusted deputy, Dr. Hugo Eckener. It took some time to regain financial footing following Germany's defeat, but Dr. Eckener's charismatic personality and business acumen resulted in the launching of a great new airship in 1928, the LZ 127 *Graf Zeppelin*. Nearly 800 feet long, the giant dirigible accommodated 20 passengers in fabulous style. Ten cabins, each with two sleeping berths, were located at the rear of a long gondola. The control rooms were at the front, and an elegant lounge area, where sumptuous meals were served, was in the middle. Over its nine-year career, the legendary Graf Zeppelin made 590 flights including a headline-making around-the-world voyage in 1929. It inaugurated regular air service between Germany and South America, and safely carried over 13,000 passengers more than a million accident-free miles.

But Eckener envisioned even grander airships to compete with the luxury ocean liners which plied the North Atlantic. Work began on the first of the new Zeppelins in 1931, and a maiden flight took place on March 4, 1936. The LZ 129 was christened *Hindenburg* in honor of Germany's late president, Paul von Hindenburg. The enormous ship was 804 feet long and 135 feet in diameter. Over 7,000,000 cubic feet of hydrogen lifted the 242-ton dirigible, while four 1,320 hp Daimler-Benz diesel engines pushed it through the air at 80 mph. The engines were housed in gondolas, two on either side, while a control car hung from the nose. Leaving Germany on May 6, 1936, the inaugural voyage to New York, with a landing at Lakehurst, New Jersey, was made in just 61 hours —half the time of the swiftest ocean liners.

The Hindenburg could accommodate up to 72 passengers (and 50 to 60 crew members) in unrivaled splendor with no noise or vibration. The two main decks were located in the ship's belly. Travelers enjoyed twin promenades with downward-looking windows and cushioned seats. A spacious dining room served the finest cuisine, and a comfortable lounge featured a specially-made baby grand piano. There were 35 passenger cabins, a reading and writing room, and a cozy smoking room (pressurized to prevent the entry of any flammable hydrogen gas). Stewards were available to cater to every whim, and the chefs prepared gourmet meals in a fully electric kitchen. The officers and crew had their own mess and sleeping quarters, and there was even a shower on board.

Operated by the new government-owned Deutsche Zeppelin Reederei (DZR), the Hindenburg made ten roundtrips across the North Atlantic in 1936, plus eight crossings to South America. On May 6, 1937, while landing at Lakehurst, the Zeppelin's hydrogen gas was somehow ignited. The huge ship exploded and fell to the ground in a pillar of flames and smoke. Incredibly, 62 of the 97 people on board escaped the inferno. But the nightmarish scene, captured on newsreel films and in countless newspaper photographs, brought the short reign of the flying leviathans to a precipitous close.

Chapter 14
Boeing 307 Stratoliner

When the airline quintet that sponsored the Douglas DC-4E published specifications for a new "Superliner," they were demanding more than increased speed, payload, and range. They wanted a transport that could fly higher, too. Why? Because while the interior appointments of airliners such as the DC-3 were luxurious, airsickness was still an all too common affliction of airline passengers. Bad weather and turbulent air at lower altitudes could bounce a plane around much like a ship on a stormy sea. So pilots faced a dilemma. Fly too low — even in good weather — and air pockets could produce airsickness. Fly too high — above the weather and over 10,000 feet — in the unpressurized cabins of the day, and passengers would be susceptible to altitude sickness, a result of the decreased oxygen content of the thin air.

Aircraft engines also encounter oxygen deprivation at higher altitudes. Although airplanes fly faster and more smoothly as they climb higher and higher, their engines

One of TWA's Boeing 307 Stratoliners seen during an early test flight. The Stratoliner was the first pressurized airliner. (Boeing)

lose power in the thin air. This problem challenged engine designers and aeronautical engineers alike. How could it be overcome?

The solution was a turbo supercharger, a device invented and first tested by Dr. Sanford Alexander Moss atop Pike's Peak, Colorado, in 1917. A turbo supercharger uses exhaust gases from an internal combustion engine to drive a turbine which compresses fresh air and then feeds it back into the engine. Aircraft engines equipped with the device operate as efficiently at higher altitudes as at sea level. And high-flying airliners, equipped with turbo superchargers, can fly farther and faster because the thinner air offers less resistance to wings and fuselage. Dr. Moss attached his invention to a Liberty aircraft engine, and the results were encouraging, though not entirely successful.

After many years of research and development work, Moss, who went to work for General Electric, finally produced a practical turbo supercharger during the mid-1930s. Boeing's engineers had two immediate uses for the device. One was a high altitude bomber they called the Model 299 which would eventually become the famous B-17 Flying Fortress. The other was a pressurized airliner, the four-engine Model 307 Stratoliner.

Work on the Model 299 began in 1934 and was based on a US Army Air Corps requirement. The following year, the prototype B-17 flew for the first time. It was an impressive machine, and the Army quickly ordered the plane into production. In December 1935, Boeing engineers began work on the Stratoliner. A key element of the design was that it shared the B-17's wing and tail assemblies as well as its Wright Cyclone engines, which were equipped with turbo superchargers. However, the Stratoliner had a completely new fuselage, resembling a big, fat cigar. Its circular cross section was best suited to the structural problems associated with pressurized cabins.

Production of the Stratoliner did not begin until 1937 when Pan American and TWA placed the first orders for four and six aircraft respectively. The prototype made its maiden flight on December 31, 1938. During a demonstration flight on March 18, 1939, this plane crashed, leading to a number of modifications to the Stratoliner's wing and tail design. Airplanes were becoming increasingly complex, and their development and flight test phases were becoming longer and more involved. The second Stratoliner resumed flight in May, and the first airline deliveries began a year later. Pan Am inaugurated service to Mexico City on July 4, 1940, and TWA followed with New York to Los Angeles flights on July 8. The flight time across the country was now reduced to 13 hours at 222 mph and 19,000 feet—well above the roughest air.

The airlines introduced the Stratoliner with a great deal of fanfare. It was, after all, the most modern airliner in the skies. It was spacious as well. By day it carried 33 passengers in deeply cushioned seats, and at night it could accommodate 16 passengers in sleeping berths and another nine in chaise-lounge chairs. Bright colors and plush carpeting decorated the cabin. Soundproofing and air conditioning as well as a full galley with fine meals contributed to the Stratoliner's reputation for luxury.

A Pan Am Stratoliner is seen over Mt. Rainier during an early test flight. Pan Am flew the Stratoliners from the southern US to Mexico City and other destinations in Latin America. (Pan American Airlines)

Pan Am and TWA each reduced their Stratoliner orders by one aircraft, Pan Am taking three and TWA, five. Another was built as an executive aircraft for TWA's new owner, the millionaire airman Howard Hughes, bringing the total to ten, including the prototype. Dubbed "The Flying Penthouse" by Hughes, he intended to use his Stratoliner to beat his own 1938 globe-girdling record flight. But those plans were abandoned when America entered World War II on December 7, 1941. Likewise, Pan Am and TWA had to change their plans when their Stratoliners were pressed into the war effort as military transports, with TWA's designated C-75s. The Stratoliners were popular with VIPs, carrying such notables as General Eisenhower, Prime Minister Winston Churchill, and Queen Wilhelmina of the Netherlands.

TWA's Stratoliners were returned to the carrier in 1944, although they required extensive overhaul and modification before they could resume commercial service. The work was completed the following year, and when the Stratoliners started flying paying passengers again on April 1, 1945, they were the world's only four-engine commercial transports. TWA kept the big planes in its fleet for another five years, during which a new generation of postwar airliners was making them obsolete. Pan Am sold its Stratoliners in 1948. Most of the secondhand airplanes wound up in Indochina, where a few continued flying well into the 1960s, with a generally good record of service. The only Stratoliner still in existence is owned by the Smithsonian's National Air and Space Museum and is now at the Museum of Flight in Seattle.

Though produced in small numbers, the Stratoliner had a considerable impact on aviation. By pioneering pressurized cabins, it paved the way for even bigger postwar airliners as well as the jetliners that followed. The high-flying Boeing 307 pointed the way to the Boeing 707 and thus to the Jet Age.

Chapter 15
Lockheed Constellation

Howard Hughes has often been portrayed as an eccentric billionaire who led a very unusual life, and it is true that as he grew older, his eccentricities became more apparent and more extreme. But this popular image implicitly forgets that Howard Hughes was both a daring pilot and a talented engineer. The son of a Texas oilman, he was born on Christmas Eve in 1905. At the age of 19, Hughes inherited his father's fortune and rapidly multiplied it. His wealth allowed him to pursue a wide range of interests, from golf to filmmaking. In 1930, he released the most expensive movie Hollywood had produced up to that time. *Hell's Angels* was a film about the exploits of World War I aviators. A box office smash, it put Hughes on the map as one of Hollywood's most talented young producer-directors. He was only 25 years old.

Hughes' interest in aviation was inspired by *Hell's Angels.* While shooting the film, he learned to fly. During the summer of 1932, he adopted a pseudonym and took a job as a pilot, flying Fokker Trimotors for American Airlines. Soon he was designing his own racing planes, setting speed records and earning aviation's top trophies. His H-1 set the world's absolute speed record in 1935, and his around-the-world flight in 1938 broke more records and earned more awards. His Hughes Aircraft Company later built the world's biggest airplane — the famous Hercules Flying Boat, also known as the *Spruce Goose*. In the ensuing years the firm produced helicopters, guided missiles, spacecraft, and satellites.

In 1939, Howard Hughes gained a controlling interest in Transcontinental & Western Air, Inc. (TWA), the predecessor company to Trans World Airlines. At the time, TWA was anticipating delivery of Boeing Stratoliners. Hughes, however, demanded even greater capabilities than those of this state-of-the-art airliner. Knowing that Lockheed had built the Model 14 he had used in his record-setting trip the year before, he and TWA's president, Jack Frye, traveled to Lockheed's headquarters in Burbank. There they met with Lockheed's president, Bob Gross, and the company's brilliant design team of Kelly Johnson and Hall Hibbard. By the summer of 1939, Lockheed submitted its proposal to Hughes and TWA. The Model 049 was called the Constellation because it incorporated so many of the successful concepts introduced in Lockheed's earlier Winged Star designs — in fact, a whole "constellation" of stellar ideas!

The new airplane was a four-engine triple-tail design somewhat reminiscent of the Douglas DC-4E. But it would be faster, carrying 40 to 60 passengers from coast to coast in less than ten hours at over 300 mph. Like the Stratoliner, it was pressurized, in addition to featuring the most modern interior appointments ever incorporated into an airliner.

Hughes was influential in determining the Constellation's final configuration. He called for numerous design changes in the cockpit and cabin, many of which frustrated

A TWA Constellation is seen in postwar colors as it appeared when service was initiated in 1946. This is an early Model 049. (Lockheed)

Lockheed engineers. Yet some of his ideas were quite practical. At any rate, no one seemed disposed to disagree with him since he was paying for the 40 Constellations TWA had ordered in 1940.

World War II intervened, and when the Constellation made its first flight on January 9, 1943, it was wearing an olive drab military paint scheme. Designated C-69 by the US Army, only 15 had been delivered by VJ-Day, when the production line was converted back to civil Constellations. The initial production models went to TWA and Pan American. Pan Am inaugurated the Constellation's peacetime service on trans-Atlantic flights beginning on January 20, 1946. TWA followed in early February with both domestic and trans-Atlantic flights.

TWA, however, had already set a record with the "Connie" two years earlier. On April 16, 1944, the first production Constellation was delivered — temporarily — to TWA. The next day Howard Hughes and Jack Frye flew the plane, painted in TWA colors, from Burbank to Washington, D.C. For Hughes, this was another record-breaking flight, with 2,400 miles covered in just seven hours. As a result of this flight, the Constellation made headlines, and the public was given a preview of what to expect in airline travel after the war. But when it arrived in Washington, the Constellation was turned over to the military. That same month, Orville Wright was given a demonstration flight aboard a Constellation. This was the last time that the world's first aviator took the controls of an airplane. Wright was impressed not only by the Constellation's performance but also by the fact that the plane's wing was longer than his first flight at Kitty Hawk. Aeronautical science had come a very long way in 40 years.

The Constellation was an immediate success when introduced into commercial service after the war. Airlines around the world began placing orders for Lockheed's latest marvel. Douglas responded with a newly designed airliner, the DC-6, launching a competition between the two companies which would continue for nearly a decade. Lockheed's Super Constellation entered service in 1951 with new engines and a stretched fuselage. The Super Constellation flew faster, farther, and higher and boasted an even more luxurious interior then previous airliners. The Super G Constellation came next,

A TWA Super Constellation over the Grand Canyon. This stretched version of the original Constellation was popular with airlines and passengers alike. (Lockheed)

The L-1649A was the final evolution of the Lockheed Constellation. The new model featured a new straight wing and was able to fly nonstop from California to Europe. This view shows the airliner's porpoise-shaped fuselage and distinctive triple-tail to advantage. (Lockheed)

in 1955, with weather radar and optional wingtip fuel tanks. The last of the breed—the L-1649A Starliner—was introduced in 1957. Featuring a new wing, the Starliner could fly nonstop from California across the North Pole to Europe. In the Starliner and the Douglas DC-7C, the piston engine airliner reached its zenith. The next step would be jet power.

But the Constellation represented more than a transition from propellers to jets. It made regular trans-Atlantic air travel and nonstop coast to coast travel a reality. In the process, ships and trains began to lose passengers to airplanes. It was a trend produced not only by increasing speeds but also by the increasing safety and reliability of modern airliners such as the Lockheed Constellation.

Hundreds of Constellations were produced, including two presidential aircraft for Dwight Eisenhower. Today, only a handful still exist. But the Constellation's beautiful porpoise-shaped fuselage and elegant triple-tail made it one of the most distinctive airliners ever to grace the skies.

Chapter 16
Douglas DC-6 and DC-7

The 1950s are often referred to as the Golden Age of propeller-driven airliners. Safe, comfortable, reliable and able to fly at relatively high speed, they made long-distance air transportation a practical undertaking. While European manufacturers made a number of attempts to meet the growing airline demand for modern aircraft, the real competition was waged between Lockheed and Douglas, two southern California companies, to build the biggest, fastest, most luxurious, and longest-ranged transports.

Lockheed had entered the fray with its triple-tailed Constellations. Douglas, which had earned fame with its classic DC-3, fought back with the DC-6 and DC-7. In terms of total numbers sold as well as aircraft still in service, Douglas would eventually come out on top. Figuring in the stories of both companies was that enigmatic billionaire, Howard Hughes.

When Douglas abandoned the DC-4E project before the war, Hughes was already working with Lockheed engineers on the more advanced Constellation. When World

A DC-6B in United Airlines service on the ground in this wintry scene. United's DC-6Bs remained in service until replaced by 737s in 1968. (United Airlines)

War II intervened, Douglas quickly developed a simpler DC-4 design for use as a military transport, designated the C-54. Lockheed was considerably slower in placing the Constellation into military service. But by the end of the war, Douglas had fallen behind its Burbank competitor in the aviation technology which fed airliner design. Unlike the Constellation, the DC-4 was unpressurized. Thus, when the DC-4 and Constellation were finally able to enter airline service after the war, Lockheed had the superior aircraft and a business advantage. However, thanks to Howard Hughes, Douglas was able to overcome Lockheed's lead.

To get the jump on his competitors at the end of the war, Hughes, as the owner of TWA, had negotiated a contract which gave his airline the rights to Lockheed's first civilian deliveries. This agreement gave Douglas the time to develop its XC-112A, an enlarged, improved, and pressurized version of the DC-4. On February 15, 1946, the same day TWA put the Constellation into commercial service, the XC-112A made its maiden flight from Santa Monica. The airliner version was named the DC-6. Airlines turned to Douglas when Hughes and TWA held up the Constellation just as they had when United cornered the market on Boeing's 247 in the early 1930s. Several placed large orders for the DC-6, and others would follow. The first DC-6 flew on July 29, 1946.

When it entered service more than a year after the Constellation, in April 1947, the Douglas DC-6 set new standards for speed and comfort. Its four Pratt & Whitney engines drove the plane at over 300 mph, considerably faster than the DC-4. Its longer pressurized fuselage accommodated 68 passengers in deeply cushioned seats. Sleeper versions were available for long-range flights. Large rectangular windows provided excellent views of the passing scenery, and a modern galley offered piping hot meals.

Unfortunately, in October 1947, catastrophe struck the DC-6. A United DC-6 caught fire and crashed in Utah, killing all 52 people on board. A few days later, an American DC-6 experienced a similar fire but managed to land safely. The conflagrations were traced to a defect in the fuel transfer system. Both airlines grounded their new DC-6 fleets for several months to repair the problem.

Approximately 175 standard DC-6s were built, in addition to 77 DC-6As, an all-cargo model featuring more powerful engines and a fuselage stretched by five feet. Another 167 DC-6As were delivered to the US Air Force and Navy as C 118s and R6D Liftmasters. With another foot added to the DC-6A fuselage, this high-performance version was known as the DC-6B in its passenger-carrying mode. The DC-6B proved to be the most popular model with a production run of 286 aircraft. It entered service in early 1951 and represented a response to Lockheed's Super Constellation. Soon every US carrier except TWA was flying the DC-6B. Airline executives who had to pay attention to the bottom line liked its low operating costs.

The DC-7 was based on the DC-6B and incorporated advanced Wright Turbo Compound engines for even greater speed as well as another fuselage stretch, allowing accommodation of up to 95 passengers. The first of 120 DC-7s took to the air on May

An American Airlines DC-6 in flight. Overcoming an early problem with fires, the DC-6 went on to become a workhorse of the airways during the 1950s. (American Airlines)

18, 1953. The following year, DC-7s gave travelers their first nonstop coast to coast service, flying from California to New York in 7 ½ hours. A popular spot on board the new planes was the rear lounge where passengers could play cards or engage in conversation. Another 96 DC-7s were completed as DC-7Bs for overseas routes. The DC-7B entered service in mid-1955, but it did not possess true intercontinental range. As a result, a final version, the DC-7C, dubbed the "Seven Seas," was flown at the end of that year.

The DC-7C incorporated longer wings, one more fuselage stretch, upgraded Wright engines, weather radar in the nose, increased fuel capacity, a taller tail, and a number of other improvements. It carried 105 passengers more than 4,000 miles at over 360 mph. Although 120 DC-7Cs were manufactured, the airplane did not gain the success enjoyed by the DC-6 series. The DC-7's big Wright engines were not only powerful, but they were also complex and very costly to operate and maintain. Once jetliners became available, the DC-7s quickly disappeared from passenger routes.

An American Airlines DC-7 cruises over the clouds. The model represented the zenith of piston-powered airliners. (American Airlines)

There is one more connection with Howard Hughes in the story of these airliners. A DC-6A was tentatively sold by Douglas to three different airlines but never delivered to any. Hughes bought the plane, towed it from the Douglas ramp at Santa Monica to the other side of the field, and let it rest there for the next 15 years. Then he had the DC-6 rolled inside a hangar where it was guarded night and day. The airplane reappeared a year later, completely restored. He then gave it away — without ever having flown it!

The DC-6 and DC-7 series were produced through 1958, the same year that their jet-powered successor, the DC-8, made its first flight. The Boeing 707 had entered service just as the last pistonliners left the production line. It is a tribute to the DC-6 that it remained in front line service for nearly another decade. Forty years after its first flight, the pleasant drone of DC-6 engines could still be heard flying overhead. What began as the DC-4E prototype in 1938 had become another classic Douglas airliner.

The XC-97 was the first postwar airplane to benefit from the B-29, and was an intermediate stage in the design evolution of the Stratocruiser. The XC-97 was envisioned as a very large troop and cargo transport. The wings, engines, landing gear and tail of the B-29 were mated to a new high-strength, double-bubble or "figure-eight" fuselage in much the same fashion as the prewar Boeing 307 Stratoliner had been built around the B-17. The first XC-97 was flown in November 1944, and in March 1947 the more advanced YC-97A versions took to the air. These improved models included features which had been built into the new B-50 bomber, itself an improved version of the B-29. The production model was designated C-97.

When the government cancelled orders for more than 5,000 B-29s at the close of World War II, Boeing received new orders from the US Air Force for a substantially smaller number of B-50s and C-97s. Eventually Boeing would deliver 888 C-97 Stratofreighters, many of them as KC-97 tankers for in-flight refuelling of long-range bombers. But at a time when Douglas and Lockheed production lines were busy churning out new airliners, Boeing was anxious to return to the civilian market so that its revenues would not be excessively dependent on government contracts.

To be competitive for the major airlines' business, Boeing would have to produce an airplane with considerably better performance than that of the DC-6s and Constellations which were dominating the skies in the years immediately following World War II. Intercontinental air traffic was mushrooming, and there was a demand for a larger, more comfortable airliner on transoceanic routes. Boeing's response was the Model 377 Stratocruiser, based on the successful C-97.

The company's new president, William M. Allen, committed the Stratocruiser to production shortly after taking the company's helm in September 1945. The prototype made its first flight on July 8, 1947. Pan American, which had flown the 314 Clipper and 307 Stratoliner before the war — and which would be the launch customer for both the Boeing 707 and 747 — placed the first order (for 20 aircraft) in June 1946. Several other airlines, including American, BOAC, Northwest, and United, placed additional orders for a total of 55 aircraft.

Pan American inaugurated Stratocruiser service on September 7, 1948. The Stratocruiser was a double-decker with seating for up to 81 passengers in the upper cabin in addition to a 14-seat lounge and bar below. On long distance flights, 28 sleeping berths were available in the forward cabin. Seating could be rapidly reconfigured as required for a particular route.

The Stratocruiser soon became a favorite among global air clientele. Passengers loved the spiral stair case leading to the popular lounge, and pilots praised the roomy flight deck with its huge wraparound windshield. The Stratocruiser was also known for promotions such as weekly "Strato Fashion Flights" on Northwest's Wednesday afternoon trips between Chicago and Minneapolis. Passengers were treated to lunch and an in-flight fashion show!

A Boeing 377 Stratocruiser in flight in Boeing colors. The airliner's "double bubble" fuselage allowed for a wider cabin, greater cargo capacity, and a popular "downstairs" lounge. (Boeing)

Despite its popularity, the Stratocruiser failed to gain additional airline orders beyond those won early in its career. The reasons for its commercial failure were varied but included the airplane's big, 3500 hp, 28-cylinder Pratt & Whitney engines, which were both temperamental and costly to operate. A number of other problems also took a great deal of time and money to remedy. Time, in fact, was the Stratocruiser's biggest problem — it had simply arrived on the scene too late. By 1960, the glamorous, though bulky, airplanes had all but vanished from the world's major air routes although not from the skies.

A few of the old "Strats" were modified to carry large, outsized payloads. Fitted with bulbous new fuselages and turboprop engines, these airplanes were dubbed "Guppies" and became indispensable during the Apollo program when they were used to carry spacecraft and rocket stages across the country. They also became invaluable to Airbus Industrie, the European aircraft consortium. With plants in Germany, France, and England, Airbus found that Guppies offered a practical means of transporting prefabricated fuselage sections and wings to the firm's jumbo jet assembly plant at Toulouse. This led some to say that it takes a jumbo to make a jumbo! Despite the relatively small number built, the Stratocruiser had a big impact on postwar air transport.

Chapter 18
Convair-Liners 240–640

At the end of World War II, most of America's airlines were still flying DC-3s in mainline service. By that time, the basic DC-3 design was more than ten years old, and though reliable, it was outdated. Change had come quickly with the introduction of the DC-6 and Constellation, with their ability to fly long-range routes. The DC-3 soon found itself relegated by the new airliners to short- and medium-range routes. Passengers, however, expected the same level of speed and comfort on these shorter flights that they had become accustomed to on the new postwar airliners. These expectations created a demand for a twin-engine medium-range medium-capacity aircraft. This requirement became known throughout the airline industry as the "DC-3 replacement." Convair's engineers were among the first to attempt a design for a potentially lucrative replacement for the DC-3.

This interior view of a North Central Convair 580 shows off the airliner's comfortable cabin. Today's commuter travelers would appreciate the extra elbow room offered by the Convairs.
(Bill Mellberg collection)

The Convair 580 made its first scheduled flights for Frontier Airlines in 1964.
(Bill Mellberg collection)

Convair had been known mostly for its large seaplanes as well as for the B-24 Liberator bomber which was produced in large numbers during the war. In 1943, the Consolidated and Vultee aircraft companies merged, later adopting the abbreviated trade name Convair. After the war, Convair's biggest project was the development and production of the giant, ten-engine B-36 strategic bomber. However, Convair was concerned, like other manufacturers, with becoming overly dependent on military contracts and sought to develop its commercial business. The Model 110, a sleek 30-seat airliner, first flew on July 8, 1946. It was long on speed but short on range and payload. Convair had designed the 110 with little input from the airlines, and as a result, no orders were forthcoming. The one and only example was scrapped and forgotten.

But the company was not ready to abandon the idea of a new twin-engine airliner. So, drawing on suggestions from the airline industry, Convair engineers came up with another design, the Convair 240. This model offered greater range and seating for up to 40 passengers in a roomy cabin. The prototype took off on its maiden flight from San Diego on March 16, 1947. Making a very favorable impression on the airlines, it was

A Convair 580 arrives at Wausau's Central Wisconsin Airport in 1980. Republic Airlines operated a large fleet of Convair 580s, mostly in the Great Lakes region of the US. (Bill Mellberg)

placed into production the following year. By the time the 240 entered service with American Airlines on June 1, 1948, more than 150 of the total production run of 176 had already been ordered by carriers around the world. In addition to these civilian aircraft, Convair built nearly 400 military models.

The popularity of the "Convair," as the airplane was more commonly known, led to successive development of improved models. The Convair 340 incorporated upgraded engines, longer wings, and a stretched fuselage with seating for 44 passengers. The first of 311 Convair 340s was delivered to United Airlines on March 28, 1952. Then came the Convair 440, first flown on October 6, 1955. Dubbed the "Metropolitan," it could accommodate up to 52 passengers and included improved cabin soundproofing and weather radar in the nose. The radome gave the airplane a sleeker appearance and enabled pilots to fly at lower altitudes and around bad weather. Over 180 Convair 440s were produced for a total of 668 Convair airliner models.

The Convair's design included four-abreast seating and integral airstairs. These stairs unfolded when the clamshell entrance door was opened, saving time on short runs by eliminating the need for stairs to be brought up to the plane. The Convair's pressurized fuselage and the 440's cruising speed of almost 300 mph made the airliner a passenger favorite as well.

By the early 1960s, Convairs were replacing the secondhand DC-3s being flown by local service carriers such as Ozark, Allegheny, and North Central. The airplanes were being used on more and more routes and seemed to have a long life ahead of them. In an effort to improve their performance and extend their lives even further, the first of a series of turboprop conversions for civilian Convairs was flown on February 9, 1955. Replacing the piston engines with British Eland engines built by the Napier firm, the Convair 340 became a Convair 540. Similar use was made of Allison 501 engines for the Convair 580 and of Rolls-Royce Darts for the Convair 600 and 640 programs.

The first Convair 580 entered service with Frontier Airlines in 1964. North Central and Allegheny had their entire fleets of Convairs converted to 580s. Texas International flew a large fleet of Convair 600s. Several other operators around the world flew turbo-prop Convairs, including the Royal Canadian Air Force. The new turboprops provided increased speed and reduced noise and vibration. They were also more economical than their piston predecessors.

As Convairs went through the conversion process, they were given complete over-hauls in addition to engine replacements. Their fuselages were strengthened so that they could safely accommodate the additional speed and power offered by the turboprops. New avionics were installed in the cockpits, and the cabins were modernized with new seats and brighter colors. The turboprop Convairs were like new airplanes, but built at a fraction of the cost.

The Convair-Liners were among the most popular transports ever built. They were especially well-liked by commuter passengers who flew them on a regular basis between city pairs such as Chicago and Detroit. While their numbers are shrinking, Convairs are still in service with a handful of airlines scattered around the globe and are likely to remain flying for some years to come. Overcoming the initial failure of the Model 110, the Convair has endured to become one of history's most successful airliners.

Unfortunately, Convair did not do as well when the company attempted to enter the Jet Age in the early 1960s. Like the Model 110, its 880 and 990 jetliners were sleek and fast. Sadly, like the 110, they were also commercial failures. In fact, as a result of the 880-990 program, Convair posted one of history's greatest corporate losses. The firm abandoned the commercial aircraft market permanently.

But the success of its 240, 340, and 440 models has made the name Convair synony-mous with air transportation for over nearly five decades. While the Convair does not enjoy the legendary status of the DC-3, it has carved its own niche in aviation history.

Chapter 19
Martin 202 and 404

Commuter air travelers in the 1950s and 1960s became familiar with a series of airliners which, like the Convairs, were produced as a model line and were often referred to by their manufacturer's name. Like their rivals, the Martin 202s and 404s were popular transports which served busy commuter air corridors as well as a variety of short-haul routes.

The Martin name is among the oldest and most respected in aviation. The firm was founded by one of America's pioneer aviators, Glenn L. Martin. In 1909, the 23 year-old Martin built and flew his own airplane, becoming the first man to fly in California. He was soon flying across the country, appearing in many air meets and exhibitions. By the time his company turned its attention exclusively to missiles and spacecraft in the early 1960s, it had produced over 12,000 airplanes.

A Northwest Martin 202 cruising over the Jefferson Memorial in Washington, DC. The crash of one of Northwest's Martins led to the discovery of a structural flaw in the wing—grounding the type for over a year. (Northwest Airlines)

Like the founders of America's other early aviation firms, Martin was an adventurer as well as an entrepreneur and had an interest in automobiles. The automobile shop he founded in 1905 financed his initial aviation ventures. By 1913, he had won an Army contract to produce training aircraft.

The first military Martins were followed by many more, including several famous bombers such as MB-2, B-10, and B-26 Marauder, and the Maryland and Baltimore bombers built for Britain's Royal Air Force during World War II. The company also manufactured Martin gun turrets for placement on other aircraft. Its last bomber design, the unorthodox but highly capable XB-51 trijet, failed to reach production when the US Air Force ordered the British-designed Canberra instead. However, Martin built the Canberra under license as the B-57 through the late 1950s.

In 1929, Martin moved his plant from Cleveland to Middle River, Maryland, near Baltimore. Five years later, the firm rolled out its most famous and beloved design, the M-130. This four-engine long-range flying boat was built for Pan American Airways' trans-Pacific route. Its name, the "China Clipper," became legend.

During World War II, Martin built even larger seaplanes, such as the PBM Mariner, for the US Navy. These flying boats were used to haul cargo, sink submarines, and rescue downed airmen. The Mariner was followed by the giant Mars and Marlin. The P6M Seamaster, which first flew in 1955, was a swept-wing jet-powered flying boat which was cancelled after only 11 had been built, ending a proud lineage.

After World War II, Martin, like other aircraft manufacturers, endured the pain of decreasing military contracts. And like other manufacturers, Martin decided to pursue the civilian market. In November 1945, the firm announced its plan to produce the Martin 202. The Martinliner was designed to seat up to 40 passengers on short- and medium-haul routes. It was unpressurized, but it did feature a then unique set of drop-down rear airstairs similar to those employed in later years on several jetliners. There was also provision for carry-on baggage, a large closet, and a full galley, all of which represented innovations for the new postwar commuter air travelers.

The Martin 202 made its first flight on November 22, 1946. It went into service in October 1947, more than half a year ahead of the competing Convair 240. Northwest Orient Airlines became the biggest customer when it purchased 25 202s. The airplane was an immediate hit with the public while the press hailed it as "the plane of the future." An additional six were built for South American operators.

Then in 1948, a basic structural flaw in the wing was recognized, and the 202s were grounded while modifications were made. The 202s could not return to service until 1950. Meanwhile, work on the pressurized 303 model was suspended in favor of the larger (also pressurized) Martin 404. The 404 first flew on October 21, 1950, and was introduced into service with TWA on October 5, 1951. Eastern Air Lines introduced the 404 the following January. By the time production ended in 1953, over one hundred

A splendid view of a Piedmont Martin 404 in flight. Piedmont was one of several local service carriers to acquire secondhand Martins. The airline served cities in the southeastern United States. (Piedmont Airlines)

404s had rolled off the line, most going to Eastern and TWA. In addition, TWA ordered a dozen 202As, which included the structural modifications that had been incorporated into previously built 202s. Altogether, 43 Martin 202s and 103 404s were produced at the Baltimore plant. They were the last airliners to bear the Martin name.

Northwest put its fleet of 202s up for sale in 1951, but Eastern and TWA flew theirs throughout the 1950s. TWA phased its Martins out in 1961. By that time, the Martins, like Convairs, were enjoying a renaissance with regional carriers such as Mohawk, Allegheny, Ozark, Pacific, Piedmont, and Southern. These airlines purchased secondhand Martins to replace DC-3s on flights to small cities such as Roanoke and Peoria. The planes proved as popular with passengers in these markets as they had been with those on bigger carriers. The 404's pressurized cabin and 44 comfortable seats received universal praise.

To the casual observer, Martins were difficult to tell apart from Convairs. They were also similar to Convairs in performance. But the structural problems that beset the 202's early career took a toll on 404 sales. Although the 202 had originally been based on American Airlines' specifications, American bought the Convair. So did United, which had shown an early interest in the Martin 303. In fact, the Martinliners were financial disasters for Glenn Martin, who passed away in 1955.

The company that bore his name went on to make valuable contributions to US space efforts. Martin's Titan rockets launched both the Gemini astronauts and the Voyager spacecraft which flew historic missions to Jupiter, Saturn, Uranus, and Neptune. Martin Marietta, the corporate entity into which Martin later merged, built the Viking spacecraft which landed on Mars in 1976. In just 25 years, Martin had gone from building piston airliners to sending spaceships to the outer planets, a reminder of how far technology had carried humanity in so brief a time. In 1995, the company joined another aerospace giant to form the Lockheed Martin Corporation.

A Martin 404 in a vintage Eastern Airlines livery. (Greenborough Associates)

Chapter 20
Avro Jetliner

On April 18, 1950, an exciting new airplane touched down at Idlewild—now re-named Kennedy International Airport in New York City. This airliner was unlike any other transport then flying in North America. For it did not have propellers. This airliner was a jetliner—in fact, *the* "Jetliner."

"Jetliner" was the name given to Avro Canada's pioneering C102, North America's first jet transport. Since it was the first jetliner to fly in the United States, its trip to New York that day made history. Although it was a test flight coming in from Avro Canada's Malton, Ontario, headquarters, the plane carried a sack of Royal Canadian Mail. That sack was the first air mail delivered by a jet transport. On hand to greet the Jetliner was an official delegation representing the Mayor of New York and a large contingent of reporters and press photographers. The Jetliner's visit made headlines all across the continent that day, and its crew was given an enthusiastic welcome to Manhattan, complete with banquet and motorcade.

The Jetliner had made its maiden flight the previous summer, on August 10, 1949. Designed by a talented group of young engineers, the airplane missed becoming the

A Jetliner taxis past a Trans Canada Air Lines DC-4M North Star at the old Malton (Toronto) terminal in 1949. The C102 represented the greatest single increase in speed of any transport ever built in North America. (National Aviation Museum)

An in-flight view of the world's second and North America's first jet transport—the Avro Canada C102 Jetliner. (Avro/George Laidlaw)

world's first jet transport by only two weeks. Britain's de Havilland Comet had made its first flight on July 27. Had the Jetliner gone into production, jet travel might well have been commonplace in North America as early as 1954—or five years ahead of the Boeing 707 and Douglas DC-8.

The Jetliner story begins with the pioneer British aviator, A.V. Roe. The company he founded in 1909, commonly known as Avro, produced many of history's most famous airplanes, from the early Avro biplanes to the bat-wing Vulcan bombers used in the Falklands conflict. Avro's best-known design was probably the World War II Lancaster bomber. More than 400 Lancasters were built in Canada by the wartime Victory Aircraft consortium.

Shortly after the war ended, Sir Roy Dobson, the head of Avro Aircraft, visited the Victory plant at Malton near Toronto. He recognized the enormous potential for aircraft development in Canada, and on December 1, 1945, A.V. Roe Canada Limited took possession of the idle Victory facility. Sir Roy assembled a brilliant team to design and build two new aircraft types. The first would be the Avro CF-100 all-weather jet interceptor for the Royal Canadian Air Force. The second project, under the leadership of

Chief Design Engineer James C. Floyd, was a short-haul jet transport for Trans-Canada Air Lines.

As Floyd and his staff began to lay out their ideas, they found themselves breaking new ground every day. The only jets flying in 1946 were military fighters, and they had been operational for less than two years. No one had built a jet airliner. It is somewhat surprising, therefore, that Jim Floyd's team encountered no major technical problems in developing the C102.

The Jetliner was a relatively simple aircraft, designed to fly over intercity routes, such as those carrying the bulk of air traffic in the United States and Canada. Its circular

Camera-shy billionaire Howard Hughes posed for C102 captain Don Rogers during the Jetliner's extended visit to California in 1952. Hughes played a role in many of the airliner stories described in this book. (Don Rogers/Jim Floyd)

pressurized fuselage could seat up to 52 passengers. There was space for a buffet and a washroom, as well as for luggage, mail, and freight. The Jetliner was not designed to compete with de Havilland's Comet, which was intended for long-range, international routes. But the Jetliner could fly higher and faster than contemporary propeller-driven airliners, such as the DC-6 and Constellation. Its four jet engines were slung in pairs under each wing. Built by Rolls-Royce, these powerplants made the Jetliner a truly revolutionary transport, a new concept in flight.

Piston-powered airliners were slow, noisy, and shaky. Flying at low altitude, they often gave a rough ride in bad weather. Jet engines offered high speed, little noise inside the cabin, and a much smoother ride at higher altitudes above the weather. The idea of jet travel in 1949 was as exciting and revolutionary to passengers then as the supersonic Concorde is to today's travelers.

Following its maiden flight, the Jetliner test program proceeded smoothly. By the end of 1950, the airplane had been cleared to carry passengers on demonstration flights. Avro lost no time in taking the Jetliner all across North America, giving airline executives the opportunity to see and experience this new concept in travel. Although the C102 had been designed around specifications set by Trans-Canada Air Lines, the carrier began to have second thoughts about the Jetliner. However, Avro was confident that a large market still existed for the Jetliner in the United States.

Consequently, the New York visit was only the first of several demonstration tours. On January 10, 1951, the Jetliner made headlines again as it broke all records on a triangular flight from Toronto to Chicago to New York and back. It flew at twice the speed — 520 mph — and twice the altitude — 36,000 feet — of contemporary propeller-driven airliners. Nearly a decade would pass before any other transport could match its performance over similar routes.

Miami-based National Airlines signed a letter of intent for four C102s with an option on six more. Howard Hughes was keen on acquiring the Jetliner for TWA, even offering to produce the airplane in the United States. But just when the Jetliner seemed to be on top of the world, the bottom fell out. The Canadian government ordered a stop to all work on the program and halted the sales effort in its tracks. The Jetliner could still be flown in conjunction with military test projects, but even those flights ended in 1956, when the C102 was cut up for scrap with only its nose being preserved for exhibit in Canada's National Aviation Museum.

What happened? The Korean War and the communist scare were looming. The government ordered Avro to allocate all of its resources to CF-100 production for the Royal Canadian Air Force. The Jetliner thus became entangled in the web of Canadian politics. As a result, the country lost a great technological lead and untold millions in export revenues. But the Jetliner represented a significant achievement and pointed the way to the future. And while it never entered production, it did lend its name to the thousands of jetliners that followed in its wake.

Chapter 21
de Havilland Comet

The story of the de Havilland Comet, the world's first jet transport, is one of aviation's great sagas. It is filled with triumph and tragedy, mystery and mastery. The Comet blazed a trail into the unknown, and along the way, this graceful airliner taught engineers some important lessons. It also introduced modern air travelers to the marvels of jet flight and made it possible for the first time to reach any point on the globe in less than two days.

The de Havilland Aircraft Company was founded by Geoffrey de Havilland in 1920. Born in England in 1882, "DH," as he was affectionately known, designed and built his first airplane in 1908. During World War I, his company produced a series of combat aircraft, each bearing the D.H. prefix. The most successful of these was the D.H.4, which was also produced in the United States. After the war, surplus D.H.4s carried US mail. In fact, shortly before his epic flight between New York and Paris, Charles Lindbergh had been an obscure air mail pilot flying D.H.4s between St. Louis and Chicago.

A Comet 4C flown by Middle East Airlines undergoes service in this 1962 airport scene.
(Bill Mellberg collection)

The first production Comet (foreground) is joined by the two prototypes in this formation flight. This aircraft's cabin later ruptured and the airliner fell into the Mediterranean on its way from Rome to London on January 10, 1954, killing all 35 people on board. (British Aerospace)

De Havilland produced the first of his famous Moth series in 1925. It was a light-weight single-engine biplane intended for the civilian market. As was the case with all of his airplanes up to 1937, DH tested the new machine himself. The D.H.60 Moth gave birth to private flying, and subsequent models established de Havilland as a world leader in aviation. De Havilland steadily earned a reputation for designing elegant airplanes, none more so than the sleek D.H.91 Albatross airliner introduced in 1937. During World War II, de Havilland was knighted for the development of his famous high-speed D.H.98 Mosquito fighter-bomber. But the Mosquito, which was nicknamed the "Wooden Wonder," cost him dearly — his test pilot son, John, was killed in one.

Looking past the war, the British government formed a committee in 1943 under the chairmanship of Lord Brabazon to anticipate the needs of a postwar civil aviation market. Several new airliner designs were recommended, including a small high-speed jet transport. De Havilland accepted the challenge of this design, and by the war's end the company was studying a number of different approaches, some quite radical. To test one of these designs, de Havilland built three small tailless D.H.108 experimental aircraft in 1946. Two years later, the Swallow would become the first British aircraft to break the sound barrier. But before that historic event, the first D.H.108 broke up during a test flight in 1946, taking the life of its pilot, Geoffrey de Havilland, Jr. The loss of another son devastated Sir Geoffrey. Yet DH carried on, despite being struck by still another tragedy: the death of his beloved wife, three years later.

The tailless concept was abandoned for the jet transport project. Instead, Chief Designer Ron Bishop chose a more conventional layout with four engines buried in moderately swept back wings. Still, the sleek lines of the jetliner were a sight to behold. The D.H.106 was appropriately named the "Comet." Built in secrecy to protect de Havilland's commercial lead, the Comet was finally revealed to the press on July 27, 1949. Early that evening, chief test pilot John Cunningham took the Comet up for its maiden flight. For civil aviation it was the beginning of the Jet Age.

A young passenger demonstrates the smoothness of jet flight by balancing match sticks on a Coke bottle in this BOAC publicity picture taken aboard a Comet 4. BOAC used many similar staged photographs during the Comet years. (British Airways)

The Comet had been produced for British Overseas Airways Corporation, which placed an initial order for 14 in 1946. Although several models were planned, the initial Comet 1 version was designed to carry 36 passengers over 1,500 miles at 500 mph. After nearly three years of exhaustive flight testing, BOAC inaugurated the world's first jetliner service on May 2, 1952. The Comet was scheduled to fly from London to Johannesburg via Rome, Beirut, Khartoum, Entebbe, and Livingstone. It created a sensation, and soon additional routes were added to BOAC's timetables. Other airlines also put the Comet into service, including U.A.T. and Air France. Additional orders soon came from Canada, Japan, and the United States. The longer-range, 44-seat Comet 2 made its first flight during the same year and seemed to auger even greater success.

De Havilland had scored a triumph for Britain. The Comet was in service more than six years ahead of its nearest American rival. With plans for the stretched, 78-seat, trans-Atlantic Comet 3 well underway, the future looked very bright indeed for de Havilland. But three accidents marred the first year's operations. Two takeoff crashes were attributed to pilot error, and another Comet broke up in a storm near Calcutta on May 2, 1953. None of these accidents was blamed on the Comet itself.

But on January 10, 1954, everything changed when a BOAC Comet crashed into the Mediterranean shortly after taking off in good weather from Rome. Several modifications were made, grounding the Comet fleet for two months. Then, just two weeks after resuming operations, another Comet crashed near Naples under nearly identical circumstances. The airplane had disintegrated in flight, and the Comet was grounded once again—permanently.

The mysterious crashes led to a lengthy investigation which revealed a new and deadly phenomenon, metal fatigue. The problem was the result of repeatedly pressurizing the cabin for high altitude flights. Tiny stress cracks formed around the window frames, and without warning, the structure could suddenly fail, leading to explosive decompression of the cabin and a crash. The tragic loss of the Comets with all on board did have a positive effect. The painful lessons learned from the Comet disasters were incorporated into the design of every subsequent jetliner.

Sir Geoffrey did not lose his vision or abandon his dreams. And Britain's faith in his genius was demonstrated by BOAC's order for 19 all-new Comet 4s in 1958. On October 4, 1958, a BOAC Comet 4 made history as the first trans-Atlantic jetliner, flying from London to New York. Other carriers ordered the improved Comets although by then, Boeing and Douglas were eating heavily into de Havilland's sales. Altogether, only 113 Comets were produced, the last one retired from airline service in 1980. But Sir Geoffrey de Havilland and the Comet will always be remembered for introducing jet travel to the world.

Chapter 22
Vickers Viscount

The Jet Age was temporarily halted in the spring of 1954 when metal fatigue grounded de Havilland's spectacular new Comet. No other pure jet airliner was in service at the time, but jet power was still available on the world's air routes in the form of another popular new British airliner, the turboprop-driven Vickers Viscount. Indeed, many air travelers around the globe were introduced to the comforts of jet travel on board a Viscount. Following its introduction by British European Airways (BEA) in 1953, this four-engine medium-range transport quickly became a familiar sight at airfields through-out Europe, Africa, the Middle East, Australia, and the Americas. Passengers appreciated its speed, its huge panoramic windows, and the smooth quiet ride offered by the Viscount's Rolls-Royce Dart turboprop engines. Pilots liked the power those turbine engines pro-vided, and airline executives were impressed by their good economics.

Like the Comet, the airplane was a result of the Brabazon Committee formed dur-ing World War II. Confident of victory, the British were eager to establish a lead in postwar civil aviation technology. In addition to the Comet, the industry experts work-

Note the large panoramic passenger windows of this Vickers Viscount in Aloha Airlines colors.
(Airliners America)

A Continental Airlines Viscount 810 wearing vintage livery. (Airliners America)

ing under Lord Brabazon's chairmanship proposed a number of different designs to fill various air transport roles. One was a huge trans-Atlantic airliner, and another was a small turboprop transport for short- and medium-range routes. Bristol designed and built the giant eight-engine Brabazon for the trans-Atlantic run. A single prototype of this aerial luxury liner was built and flown before the costly and controversial project was finally abandoned in 1953.

For a time, it looked as though the smaller Vickers turboprop would share a similar fate. Having produced the famous Wellington bomber and the postwar Viking transport (which was based on the bomber design), Vickers put together a formal proposal for its "VC2" in June 1945. The following year, the design was finalized as the Type 630, and the construction of two prototypes was authorized by the Ministry of Supply. The airplane would be powered by the new Rolls-Royce Dart turboprop engine, another product of the Brabazon Committee's farsighted recommendations.

A Vickers Viscount in Capital Airlines colors. Note the pencil-like engine nacelles. (Vickers)

Dubbed the "Viceroy" until the partition of India in 1947, the Viscount was designed around its turboprop engines. The Viscount was the world's first turboprop airliner, and the first jet-powered transport to enjoy widespread use. Unlike a pure jet engine, which ejects a high-speed stream of hot gases to produce forward thrust, a turboprop (or "propjet") engine uses an extra series of turbines to harness the jet's energy. That energy is then used to drive a propeller by means of a reduction gear. A small amount of residual jet thrust is also ejected through the exhaust system. Turboprop engines are easier to maintain and more economical than piston engines. And they are more efficient than pure jets on shorter routes flown at more moderate speeds.

When the first Viscount took to the air on July 16, 1948, test pilot "Mutt" Summers described it as "the smoothest and best I have ever flown." Many other people shared his opinion after the airliner was taken to France on a demonstration tour later that year. But despite the Viscount's early promise, British European Airways, its intended customer, ordered a competing piston-powered design—the Viscount was deemed too small. It then appeared as if the Viscount design would be abandoned. But Rolls-Royce increased the power output of the Dart engine, and Vickers increased the length of the airplane's fuselage so that it could accommodate 53 passengers at a cruising speed of nearly 350 mph. This improved Type 700 model had much greater appeal, leading to BEA's initial order for 20 aircraft in August 1950. It would be followed by many more.

On April 19, 1953, BEA inaugurated the world's first regularly scheduled propjet service. The Viscount drew passengers like a magnet. They were impressed not only by the airplane's comfort but also by its picture windows, each measuring 26 inches high and 19 inches wide. The spectacular view offered by these windows was, in the words of one woman, "better than sitting at the movies." No airplane in its class could match the Viscount's performance.

In 1952, Vickers received an initial order for 15 improved models from Trans-Canada Air Lines (TCA). TCA gave the firm a long list of modifications that were required for North American service. But these proved to be well worth the engineering effort as 147 airplanes were eventually sold across the Atlantic. By 1955, Capital Airlines (later to merge with United) received the first of 60 Viscounts. People all across North America were coming to airports simply to gawk at the new airliners. With their highly polished aluminum wings, pencil-like engine nacelles, and distinctive jet whistle, the Viscounts looked fast even when they were sitting still!

The Viscount's popularity encouraged Vickers to make other improvements to the type, including a longer faster version for Continental Airlines equipped with 52 first-class seats and an intimate four-seat lounge at the rear of the cabin. These plush Viscount 810s entered service between Chicago and Los Angeles in 1958.

But the popular British airliners did not rule the skies for long. By the end of the decade, the introduction of the new American-built jetliners took much of the excitement away from the Viscount. After all, turboprops still had propellers, and the public was soon demanding pure jets even on short- and medium-range routes. Viscount production ceased in 1964 after 444 aircraft had been built, though in its place came British Aircraft Corporation's pure-jet successor — the BAC One-Eleven. Forty years after entering service, a few Viscounts were still hauling passengers. In the end, the Viscount was not only Britain's most successful airliner. It was also the airplane that changed our entire notion of air travel. It was a genuine aviation classic.

Chapter 23
Bristol Brabazon

Of the various airliner designs recommended by Britain's Committee on Postwar Civil Aircraft in 1943, only one would be named in honor of its chairman, Lord Brabazon of Tara, the first Baron of Sandwich. John Theodore Cuthbert Moore-Brabazon received his country's first pilot's certificate in 1910, flew in the Royal Air Corps during World War I, was president of the Royal Aeronautical Society from 1934 to 1936, and served as Minister of Aircraft Production during World War II. He was knighted for his distinguished career in 1942.

A lifelong aviation proponent, Lord Brabazon headed the Committee on Postwar Civil Aircraft (better known as the Brabazon Committee), which was charged with identifying postwar market needs and making recommendations to the British aircraft

The Bristol Brabazon 1 undergoing engine tests at Filton on May 6, 1952, a year before the project was cancelled. Behind it is the huge Aircraft Assembly Hall, built for the specific purpose of fabricating the giant new airliner. (British Aerospace)

industry for the development of several transport types, each designated for a specific market. Type I was listed as a large, propeller-driven, trans-Atlantic luxury liner. When the type numbers were dropped in favor of names, this flying behemoth was dubbed "Brabazon 1."

After the war, the Bristol Aeroplane Company at Filton took on the project, applying its earlier studies for a long-range bomber to the new airliner. The chief designer was A.E. Russell (later Sir Archibald), who years later played a similar role in the development of the Concorde. (Indeed, the supersonic transport was built in the same Filton hangar as the Brabazon.) But in 1945 Russell had a giant challenge after Bristol was given the go-ahead to produce two Brabazon prototypes and up to ten production models. At the time, the airliner was going to be the world's largest land-based air transport.

To produce the huge new airliner, the company first had to build an enormous new Brabazon Assembly Hall. Its three bays were each over 1,000 feet long, and covered two million square feet of floor space, making it the biggest aircraft hangar in the world. The airplane itself was 177 feet long, stood 50 feet high, and had a 230-foot wingspan. It weighed 290,000 pounds at takeoff, and was powered by eight 2,650 hp Bristol Centaurus 20 air-cooled engines driving eight paired (contra-rotating) propellers, each 16 feet in diameter. The engines were buried in the wings with only narrow propeller shafts extending from the leading edge. This arrangement reduced drag and added to the Brabazon's "clean" appearance.

Twenty years before the dawn of the "Jumbo Jet," Bristol was building a true giant. Yet, despite its size, only 80 passengers were to be carried in the Brabazon; but those lucky travelers would enjoy unmatched comfort and luxury during their nonstop, 13-hour flights between London and New York. The airplane's cabin was divided into several large compartments which featured a dining salon, lounge, and cinema. Seats could be converted into berths for sleeping, and large windows provided panoramic views of the passing scene. Brabazon service was truly going to be First Class!

Of course, such luxury came at a price, and from the outset, neither Bristol nor its government sponsors gave much thought to the Brabazon's costs. As Russell said in a BBC interview many years later, "It was obvious the cost of the ticket was going to be fabulous... I had my doubts fairly soon, but not strong enough to jump over the bridge."

It took nearly four years to get the Brabazon into the air. The challenge of designing and building such an ambitious project proved to be greater than anticipated. Then again, the airplane was a trailblazer—its new technology took civil aircraft engineering from the 1930s into the 1950s. New structures, new materials, and new systems were being tried for the first time. For example, the Brabazon was the world's first airplane to make use of fully powered flight controls. No pilot would have been strong enough to move the giant ailerons, elevators, and rudder using his own muscle!

Finally, on September 4, 1949, Bristol's chief test pilot, A.J. "Bill" Pegg, boarded the Brabazon together with nine fellow crew members for the maiden flight. On that beautiful, warm Sunday morning, thousands of spectators—including Lord Brabazon—were on hand to watch as Pegg taxied the airplane to the west end of the big runway. They heard the roar of its engines as Pegg applied full power and released the brakes. After a mere 1,500-foot takeoff roll, the airliner rose majestically into the sky, accompanied by the audible gasps and cheers of the admiring crowd. Lord Brabazon was one of the first to congratulate Pegg at the end of the successful flight. "You fly the cockpit," the pilot quipped, "and the rest comes after you!"

During the next four years, the sight and sound of the Brabazon became very familiar around Filton. With its long, graceful wing, the airplane looked magnificent in flight, and the low distinctive drone of its engines could be heard from miles away. Because of its size, the Brabazon appeared to be lumbering across the sky. In fact, at 250

The Bristol Brabazon 1 in flight over the English countryside during a test flight. Its eight engines were buried in its enormous wing with only the propeller shafts exposed, giving the airplane a remarkably clean wing. (Bristol Aircraft/George Bloomfield)

mph it *was* lumbering—which is why it had become increasingly clear that the big transport would be obsolete before it ever entered airline service.

The Brabazon's first flight took place five weeks after the de Havilland Comet's. Although the new jet did not have the Brabazon's range or capacity, it was more than twice as fast as Bristol's giant, and a trans-Atlantic version was already being developed. Speed, not size, was the trend at the time, and jumbo jets were still two decades away.

Years behind schedule, well over its cost estimates, and slower than its smaller American competitors, the Brabazon became the subject of political debate and controversy. In the end, the graceful airplane was a white elephant. The program was cancelled on July 9, 1953, and the Brabazon 1, together with an unfinished second prototype, were cut up for scrap on the hangar floor that October. Nevertheless, the Brabazon was a true harbinger of things to come, and it deserves recognition for the contributions it made to the advancement of civil aircraft engineering and technology.

Chapter 24
Fokker F.27 Friendship

Over the years, many aircraft manufacturers have set out to produce a replacement for the DC–3. Given the wide variety of roles that the DC–3 has played since it first entered service in 1936, that task is a tall order. Martin and Convair certainly did their best, yet neither succeeded completely. Others have tried, but perhaps the airliner that could most legitimately lay claim to being the heir to the DC–3's mantle of versatility is Fokker's F.27 Friendship.

It is particularly fitting that the F.27 should replace the DC–3, for it was the DC–3 and its immediate precursor, the DC–2, which replaced the famous Fokker trimotors as the predominant passenger air transports of the 1930s. The appearance of the DC–2 in 1934, with its all-metal construction and streamlined shape, sealed the fate of the wooden Fokkers on the world's airways. A shrewd businessman, Anthony H.G. Fokker in effect decided, "If you can't beat them, join them." So Fokker in that same year obtained the

The first Fairchild Hiller FH-227 in flight. This American-built version of the F.27 had a stretched fuselage and more powerful Dart engines among several features that distinguished it from the Dutch-built Friendships. (Fairchild Hiller)

licensing and sales rights for Douglas airliners in Europe. None were manufactured in Holland, but Fokker did sell a total of 39 DC-2s and 46 DC-3s.

When Fokker passed away suddenly at age 49 on December 23, 1939, his company was developing the F.XXIV, Fokker's first all-metal airliner. The Dutch government was to have subsidized the airplane's development, but World War II intervened. The F.XXIV would have been a twin-engine high-wing machine.

During the war years, the Fokker factory was occupied, like the rest of Holland, by the Nazis. The company was compelled to manufacture both parts and airplanes for the Luftwaffe although workers practiced a form of passive resistance which produced very little useful work. When the Germans fled the Allied onslaught, they stripped the plant bare. But after the war Fokker still retained a nucleus of talented people with a strong desire to get back into the business of building commercial airliners.

J.E. van Tijen, the company's pre-war director, had wisely deposited a large sum of money in the New York branch of a Canadian bank just before the Nazi invasion. After the war, that money was used to help restart the firm. Van Tijen was put back in charge after being found alive at the notorious Buchenwald concentration camp in Germany, where he had been sent following his arrest by the Gestapo in 1943.

Fokker retained its licensing rights for the DC-3 in Europe and set about overhauling and converting military C-47s into DC-3 airliners. The company also manufactured a small number of Swedish Saab 90 Scandia transports and began studying plans for its own little jetliner called the F.26 Phantom. The design was not produced although by 1950 Fokker's market research had laid the foundations for the F.27 — a "DC-3 replacement." A full-size fuselage mock-up of the F.27 was built in 1952. Drawing on the Viscount's success with the Rolls-Royce Dart turboprop, Fokker planned to mate two of these engines with a high-wing design, carrying 32 passengers on short-haul routes such as those then being served by DC-3s. The high-wing configuration provided passengers easy access on the ground as well as an outstanding view from the air.

The prototype F.27 made its first flight on November 24, 1955. Production models were lengthened to seat 44 people in a comfortable pressurized cabin. Early in 1956, Fokker signed an agreement with Fairchild to manufacture and sell the F.27 under license in the United States. The first Fairchild-built F-27 was flown on April 12, 1958 (a hyphen was used to distinguish Fairchild F-27s from Fokker F.27s). Deliveries of the new short-haul transports began later that same year with a Fairchild F-27 going to Piedmont Airlines. Aer Lingus in Ireland received the first Fokker-built F.27.

Fairchild had the sales rights for the Americas with the exception of Brazil and got off to a good start. Fokker did not do as well, and for a while it looked as though production at Amsterdam might cease. The Dutch government offered its continued support as did a consortium of banks. Fokker stood by its first airliner in two decades, and sales soon picked up. The company never looked back.

A Fokker-built F.27 flown by Mississippi Valley Airlines. Note the Friendship's long, thin wing.
(Fokker Aircraft)

Indeed, the F.27 went on to become the world's best selling turboprop airliner. Fokker developed a number of versions, as did Fairchild. The American company produced a total of 205 F-27s and FH-227s, a stretched model seating 52 passengers. When Fokker ended its 30-year production run in 1987, a total of 786 airplanes had been built for 168 customers in 63 countries, including Fairchild's licensed production. As if to prove the airplane's worth, one customer actually replaced an entire fleet of older F.27s with a new fleet of F.27s, the first time an aircraft type had replaced itself!

The success of the F.27 stemmed from its reliability and rugged construction. It was the first airliner to make extensive use of metal bonding materials instead of rivets. Like the DC-3, its performance enabled it to make use of most of the world's airports, from the biggest cities to remote jungle and desert airstrips. Its flexibility made it every bit as useful hauling freight as carrying passengers. The F.27 also served in a number of military roles.

Like the DC-3, the F.27 will continue to provide useful service over an extended period of many decades. Like the DC-3, it has taken air transportation to places that have never seen a modern airliner. And like the DC-3, it is an economical aircraft, which is why so many were sold.

That is also why the F.27 went into production in a new guise. When Fokker stopped building F.27s, it began production of the Fokker 50, described by some as "a Friendship with a face lift." The Fokker 50 is a highly developed transport based on the proven F.27 design. The last of 212 Fokker 50s was delivered in 1997, which ensures the continued use of the basic F.27 airframe well beyond the year 2000. Fokker's claim to having created a genuine DC-3 replacement is well founded, indeed. Anthony Fokker, the Flying Dutchman, would have been pleased by the Friendship's enviable record.

An Ozark Air Lines FH-227B making a brief stop at Champaign, Illinois in 1971. The airliner required little service between flights, permitting quick turnarounds on multi-stop regional airline routes. (Bill Mellberg)

Chapter 25
Lockheed L-188 Electra

Few airliners have generated as much excitement as did the Vickers Viscount following its introduction in 1953. The world's first turboprop airliner was especially popular in the United States where Capital Airlines challenged its larger competitors by offering jet-powered flights between major cities. The Viscount's success did not go unnoticed by carriers such as American and Eastern Air Lines. But it was too small to replace their bigger, though slower, DC-6Bs and Constellations.

American Airlines had, in fact, issued a requirement for a new medium-range prop-jet in 1954. Such an airplane was needed for intercity routes, including those intended for the Viscount. But American wanted a propjet transport with a significantly greater range and payload than the British airliner could offer. Eastern had a similar requirement, and Lockheed engineers soon responded by offering a design that could carry

A brand new Electra in American Airlines colors at Lockheed's Burbank plant. This view shows off the airplane's stubby wings and huge propellers. (American Airlines)

An Eastern Air Lines Electra in the carrier's "hockey stick" markings. At the time this photograph was taken, the Electra was being used primarily on Eastern's short-range shuttle flights.
(Eastern Airlines)

twice as many passengers as the Viscount. It was given a company model number, L-188, and dubbed "Electra" after its famous ancestor, the highly successful Model 10 airliner.

American Airlines placed an order for 35 of the new Electras on June 8, 1955. Eastern ordered 40 of its own three months later. By the time of its first flight on December 6, 1957, 144 Electras had been ordered by nearly a dozen airlines worldwide. The program was off to a good start.

The Lockheed Electra attracted a lot of attention with its impressive 13½-foot diameter four-bladed Aeroproducts propellers, each driven by a powerful Allison 501-D13 engine which was similar to those used on Lockheed's C-130 cargo transport. The highly efficient wing looked stubby compared to those of other airplanes. As one pilot asked, "Where is it?" But the Electra's wing was designed to take advantage of the 54 feet of propeller slipstream blowing over the airfoil. This combination of wing, engine, and propeller gave the airplane built-in lift and a cruising speed greater than 400 mph. It would also be the focus of future controversy—and tragedy.

The test program proceeded smoothly from Lockheed's Burbank plant as well as from its flight development center at Palmdale, California. During 1958, additional orders came in from Australia and Northwest Orient Airlines. Late in the year, the Electra went on an around-the-world sales tour. The trip was completed without a single mechanical failure or malfunction. Eastern Air Lines inaugurated the first Electra service on January 12, 1959, followed by American ten days later. The airplane seemed to have something for everyone.

The Electra was a pilot's airplane with plenty of power, outstanding performance, and a large roomy cockpit. Passengers appreciated the wide cabin, plush seats, and rear lounge. And the airplane's economics pleased airline executives with an eye on the bottom line. Designed to carry 99 passengers, the Electra could make money carrying only 50. There was every reason to believe that Lockheed would sell hundreds of airplanes.

But then disaster struck. On the night of September 29, 1959, a brand new Braniff International Airways Electra crashed halfway between Houston and Dallas near the tiny town of Buffalo, Texas. An American Airlines Electra had crashed the previous February while landing at New York's La Guardia Airport, an accident which had been attributed to pilot error. This crash was different. The left wing and its engines were found a mile

An American Airlines Lockheed Electra in flight. The three small windows at the rear of the aircraft mark the position of the aft lounge. (American Airlines)

and a half from the wreckage of the fuselage. It was obvious that the airplane had been torn apart in flight. What was not so obvious was the cause. The possibilities included sabotage and structural failure.

Less than six months later, on March 17, 1960, another Electra crashed near Tell City, Indiana. This was a Northwest flight traversing the Chicago to Miami route. Like the Braniff crash, one of the wings—this time the right one—was found two miles from the fuselage. Clearly, something was wrong with the Electra, and critics demanded that the airplane be grounded. But, linking the problem to the airplane's high speed, the Federal Aviation Administration simply placed restrictions on how fast pilots could fly the Electra until the mystery was solved.

Following an exhaustive investigation, the problem was traced two months later to a phenomenon called "whirl mode," which is a form of vibration related to the gyroscopic effects of a propeller. A slight nudge to a child's gyroscope makes it wobble. Likewise, a small air pocket is enough to cause the same aberrant behavior in a propeller although the engine mounts usually absorb the motion and dampen the vibration. But the outboard engine mounts in the two Electras which crashed were defective, and the vibrations increased to the point where the wings were ripped from the fuselage. Lockheed devised a modification program to strengthen the Electra's wings and engine mounts. This eliminated the danger, and the airplane was given a clean bill of health and permission to resume high-speed flight.

Unfortunately, two more Electras crashed during 1960. Although neither accident was attributable to the aircraft itself, the torrent of bad publicity generated by the string of crashes scared passengers away from the Electra. Even some pilots refused to fly the type. Only a handful of additional orders were received, and Lockheed ended up producing just 170 planes. The Electra's demise was a result not only of its notorious reputation but also of the growing demand for pure jets on medium-range routes. By the time the last Electra was sold in 1960, France's elegant Caravelle was already in service, and Britain was working on the BAC One-Eleven. But the Electra continued to provide yeoman service on high-density shuttle routes for many years. Its problems resolved, the Electra managed to regain favor with the traveling public. The basic design achieved great success in military guise as the P-3 Orion maritime patrol aircraft. Hundreds of Orions have served with military forces around the globe. Commercial Electras are still in use, mainly on medium-range freight runs. Despite the early disasters, Lockheed's Electra has proved to be a very reliable and most productive airliner.

Chapter 26
Vickers Vanguard

According to the old adage, if you build a better mouse trap, the world will beat a path to your door. But such was not the case with the Vickers Vanguard, an airliner which, in theory, should have been a world beater.

The Vanguard had its roots in the highly successful Viscount. Passenger reaction to the world's first turboprop airliner was extremely positive, so it is not surprising that Vickers was soon planning a larger successor. They were not alone. Lockheed was hard at work developing its Electra, a similar four-engine propjet. But Vickers' Type 900 Vanguard—with its Rolls-Royce RB.109 Tyne engines—would carry a greater payload, fly higher and faster, and offer more economy than its American rival.

To a large extent, the Vanguard's design was closely tailored to the requirements of British European Airways (BEA), which needed an airplane for its high-density, me-

An Air Canada Vickers Vanguard during takeoff. Note the large propellers, made by de Havilland. (Air Canada)

A typical in-flight scene aboard a Trans-Canada Air Lines Vanguard shows one of the airliner's large Viscount-style windows. (Air Canada)

dium-range routes. The BEA specifications called for a transport which could seat be-tween 90 and 100 passengers (with a superior standard of comfort), cruise at 425 mph, offer very large freight holds, and provide built-in airstairs and large, "Viscount-style" windows. The first order for 20 Vanguards came from BEA on October 17, 1955 with the manufacturer also announcing that it would make every effort to attract sales from abroad, as it had done with the Viscount. The first airliners were scheduled for delivery by the spring of 1960, and Vickers promised that its Vanguards would be "ahead of all known competition in speed, reliability, economy, comfort, pilot handling, maintenance characteristics, ability to make quick turnarounds, and general passenger appeal."

Comfort was, indeed, one of the Vanguard's strong points. It made use of the Viscount's huge oval windows, which gave passengers a panoramic view of the world below. The cabin was also designed to provide exceptional head, leg, and elbow room, even in coach. The pilots had a spacious cockpit and a huge wraparound windscreen. Ground crews liked the cargo hold's clamshell doors, which made loading easy.

A Vickers Vanguard in its original Trans-Canada Air Lines colors. (Air Canada)

It was the Vanguard's large capacity freight holds that first attracted the attention of Trans-Canada Air Lines (TCA). In its search for a medium-range turbine transport to complement its planned fleet of Viscounts and Douglas DC-8 jets, TCA considered several different types. But with only a few passengers on board its "night owl" cross-country flights, the Vanguard could still earn a profit carrying freight and mail. Canada's cold winters and TCA's long-haul overwater flights to the West Indies also favored the airplane's four-engine performance and flexibility. In addition, both Vickers and Rolls-Royce had already forged positive relationships with TCA through their sales of the Viscount.

Thus, on January 3, 1957, Trans-Canada Air Lines announced that it was buying 20 Vanguards with options on four more. TCA's aircraft would be Type 952s, featuring uprated Tyne engines and a higher maximum takeoff weight than BEA's Type 951s. Cruising at 425 mph, the new Vanguard would be the fastest propeller-driven airplane ever offered in the West (the Soviet Union's Tupolev Tu-114 propjets could fly at a remarkable 478 mph). Deliveries to TCA were scheduled to begin in the fall of 1960.

Vickers' sales department forecast a potential market for 250 Vanguards worldwide, and soon work was underway at the firm's Weybridge plant southwest of London. The prototype was rolled out of its hangar on December 4, 1958. But after a short series of ground tests, its four Tyne turboprop engines were returned to Rolls-Royce at Derby. Although the Tyne was an advanced engine which promised significant improvements over the Dart, its famous predecessor (for an equivalent amount of power, it burned half as much fuel), the new engine was having more than its share of teething problems.

Finally, on January 20, 1959, the Vanguard took off on its maiden flight with Vickers' chief test pilot Jock Bryce at the controls. He described the airplane's performance as "quite sprightly." Flight testing proceeded smoothly, with the first production aircraft joining the program that April. At the same time, TCA ordered three more airplanes, and Vickers launched an aggressive new marketing campaign, demonstrating the Vanguard to a number of potential buyers.

The new propjet entered scheduled service with TCA on February 1, 1961, followed by BEA a month later (although that carrier had started using the airplane on non-scheduled flights the previous December). Passenger reaction was generally favorable, but there were some complaints about excessive noise and vibration in the forward compartment. In addition, the Tyne engines were plagued by more irksome mechanical delays. Vickers found a partial cure for the vibration, and Rolls-Royce rectified the problems with its Tynes. Once these wrinkles were ironed out, the Vanguard finally delivered on its promise. In fact, because of its low direct operating costs, TCA began offering low "economy" fares.

But in a New Year's interview at the beginning of 1961, TCA president, Gordon McGregor, predicted a limited future for the big propjets on long and medium-range routes. While he praised the Vanguard's high speed and low costs, he noted the public's growing fascination with pure jets. On most of the airline's routes, pure jets offered little advantage in speed over the Vanguard, and were more expensive to fly. However, in 1961 that made no difference to the average passenger, who considered anything with propellers to be obsolete. Although his Vanguards were brand-new, McGregor realized it was only a matter of time before he would be forced to replace them.

His words were prophetic. Air Canada (TCA's new name) took the Vanguard out of passenger service in 1971, while BEA had begun withdrawing the airliner from its fleet in 1968. Some were converted into freighters, while others went to secondhand operators. But in the end, despite its fine qualities, only 44 Vanguards were built.

Section Three
The Modern Age of Airliners
(1958–present)

This Northwest Airlines Boeing 747 demonstrates the airliner's grace in flight despite its tremendous size. (Northwest Airlines)

With the introduction of the Boeing 707 in 1958, the Jet Age had finally arrived. The era might be more accurately described as the "Turbine Revolution," since the advent of the gas turbine—or "jet"—engine revolutionized not only the airline business, but the travel industry as a whole.

The first generation of jetliners had an immediate impact on transoceanic and cross-country travel. Why spend four days aboard the *Queen Mary*, when you could fly from New York to Europe in seven hours? And why spend two days aboard the Santa Fe *Super Chief*, when you could fly from Chicago to Los Angeles in four hours? By 1960, there were 70,000 flights being made each year across the North Atlantic. Airliners were not only competing with, they were rapidly replacing ocean liners and passenger trains.

This transformation became complete with the advent of the second generation of jetliners. Beginning with the Boeing 727 in 1964, jet travel was introduced to medium-range routes. For the first time it was possible for business executives to commute between cities such as New York and Chicago. This evolution has reached a final stage today, with a new generation of regional jets and propjets which is bringing speed and comfort to even the shortest air routes.

Today, we think nothing of boarding an airliner to fly from one place to another, whether our destination is Peoria or a town halfway around the world. But before air travel could become routine, several other "revolutions" aside from airliner design were necessary. Examples include computers, which now handle everything from passenger reservations to flight management systems; and navigation satellites, which accurately guide pilots to virtually any airport in the world.

Jumbo jets, symbolized by Boeing's giant 747, have brought the world even closer together. They've made air travel far more affordable, thus influencing culture as well as commerce. A generation ago, few people could afford to visit distant lands. Now men and women travel quickly from one corner of the globe to another, enjoying a hot meal and a good movie along the way. Nearly 600 million people were carried by US airlines alone in 1997, and the numbers are growing with each passing year. In fact, passenger loads are expected to double over the next 15 years. Hopefully, the fact that more people will experience foreign culture by visiting and being visited by strangers will result in greater peace and understanding among the peoples of the world.

The rapid growth of the airline industry during the first 20 years of the Jet Age was accompanied by a number of challenges. Airports had to be expanded with new runways laid down and new terminal facilities built to handle increased traffic. The surrounding infrastructure needed to be upgraded as well, with new hotels, new highways, new office centers, new industrial parks, and new homes. Entire communities sprung up around airports, giving rise to another concern: noise pollution. Early jetliners assaulted eardrums and rattled windows for miles around. Noise is still a problem, and the aircraft industry has spent billions of dollars to produce a new generation of "good neighbor" jets. Modern airliners are still getting bigger, faster, safer, quieter…and better!

Chapter 27
Boeing 707

As the 1960s began, satellites were circling the Earth at previously unimaginable speeds and altitudes. Back on the planet's surface, meanwhile, long-distance travel was still dominated by two aging, if reliable, modes of transport: railways and ocean liners. The Douglas DC-3's legendary status had been based on its impact on culture and the world's imagination—for the first time, the public had grasped that flying would soon become a routine part of their lives. Although a harbinger of things to come, the DC-3 did not replace traditional means of travel over long distances. But the promise it had so tantalizingly offered was finally fulfilled with the arrival of the Boeing 707.

The 707 represented a turning point in transportation history. While the de Havilland Comet had launched the Jet Age, the introduction of the 707 marked the true beginning of a new age in travel. Coinciding with the dawn of the Space Age and man's march to the frontier of space, the 707 inspired airline marketing departments to concoct cosmic

An early Pan American World Airways Boeing 707 trails heavy smoke during takeoff. This was normal for the original water-injected engines which powered the airliner. (Pan American World Airways)

One of the best known 707s was Air Force One. Here President Ronald Reagan's presidential jet is seen over George Washington's home at Mount Vernon. Several different 707 models served eight presidents from Eisenhower to Bush. (White House)

nicknames for their new jetliner, such as "Astrojet" and "Star Stream." An American Airlines brochure declared, "Your plane is floating in a clear, dimensionless world of its own. On a particularly clear day you can sometimes see the very curve of the Earth's surface at the horizon. Flying over New York City at 35,000 feet…you might make out both Washington and Boston in the distance—a 400 mile span! Even the sky through which you cruise looks different. It is an incredibly dark blue, clear and deep." Travel on ocean liners and railway coaches seemed dull and outmoded in comparison.

If the 707 changed the way people thought about travel, it also changed the aircraft industry. Boeing had never enjoyed commercial success with its previous airliners. But the 707 gave birth to a "family" of transports that have since dominated the global airliner market. This domination was the payoff to one of the aviation industry's greatest gambles.

After World War II, Boeing produced a limited number of its 377 Stratocruisers for long-range airline routes. But, like the British, the company realized that gas turbine engines were the wave of the future. Boeing gained invaluable experience with large, multi-engine jet aircraft during its development of the B–47 and B–52 jet bombers for the US Air Force. The B–47 and B–52, first flown in 1947 and 1952, respectively, featured swept back wings and pod-mounted jet engines. For a time, Boeing engineers studied a jet-powered model of the Stratocruiser. But in August 1952, when Britain was leading the world with its sensational jet-powered Comet, Boeing announced that it was investing more than $16 million of its own funds in an entirely new four-engine 600 mph 180-seat jet transport. This program would culminate in the 707.

The prototype, dubbed the Model 367–80 (or "Dash Eighty"), first flew on July 15, 1954, with Boeing test pilot A. M. "Tex" Johnston at the controls. On hand for the flight was the company founder, Bill Boeing. Johnston reported that the airplane "wanted to climb like a rocket" at the beginning of its 90-minute debut. The Dash Eighty flew flawlessly on that flight and then on many, many more.

But the excitement at Boeing was not shared by everyone in the airline industry. The grounding of the Comet that spring cast a shadow over the Jet Age. Despite some

The Boeing 720 was a shortened version of the 707 with a modified wing optimized for medium-range routes. Here a 720 flown by United Air Lines is seen at Chicago's O'Hare International Airport. (Bill Mellberg)

doubters, the US Air Force soon placed its first orders for the KC–135 military tanker-transport version of the Dash Eighty. Over 800 KC-135 and related military models would eventually be produced.

Boeing proceeded to put the Dash Eighty through grueling tests to demonstrate its structural integrity and superior performance. Meanwhile, Douglas Aircraft announced its own plans for a jetliner. The DC-8 would be somewhat bigger than the 707, its wider fuselage allowing six-abreast seating and longer range. Potential customers wavered between the two types. Boeing had the advantage of being able to demonstrate a flying airplane while Douglas found it easier to make design changes with their "paper" airplane.

Finally, Pan American World Airways placed an order on October 13, 1955, for 20 707s and 25 DC-8s! The 707s would be delivered first, but these early models were better suited to transcontinental flights than the trans-Atlantic routes Pan Am was eager to serve. To get even this order, Boeing had to enlarge the 707 airframe, giving it a "double-bubble" fuselage which allowed for six-abreast seating. The airplane was also lengthened. These were expensive design changes, but they were necessary to secure additional orders from American Airlines as well as from overseas customers. Eventually, Boeing produced several 707 models as well as the medium-range 720, with differing lengths, wing configurations, and powerplants.

The introduction of Pratt & Whitney JT3D turbofan engines in 1961 provided the 707 with improved performance and economics. Turbofan engines combine the advantages of pure jets and turboprops. They use an extra compressor, or fan, which passes cold air around the engine nacelle where it is mixed with hot jet exhaust. The result is increased flow at lower temperature and velocity, making the engine more efficient, more economical, and less noisy. This last point was especially important as the loud scream of early jet engines had quickly become an issue in residential communities adjacent to major airports.

Pan Am inaugurated 707 service between New York and London on October 28, 1958. The airline also introduced the larger 707-320 Intercontinental model the following year. Meanwhile, American Airlines started flying 707s across the United States in January 1959. Coast to coast travel time was now reduced to just four and a half hours. Passengers could fly from New York to Paris in less time than it took a train to travel from Chicago to Cleveland. Their ride in a luxurious cabin was smooth, quiet, and comfortable. During the course of a year, a dozen 707s could carry as many passengers across the Atlantic as the Cunard Line's giant Queens.

This type of performance meant overwhelming competition for ocean liners and passenger trains. Indeed, the economics of jet travel would soon relegate both to secondary status when it came to long-distance transport. Boeing produced nearly one thousand 707s, setting a new standard for both business and pleasure travelers. In the process, its name became a household word in the exciting new jet era.

Chapter 28
Douglas DC-8

Starting with the DC-2 in 1934, the Douglas Aircraft Company enjoyed a 20-year reign as the world's leading manufacturer of commercial air transports. By 1954, the firm was busy producing the DC-6 and DC-7, for which Lockheed provided the main competition with its Constellation series. But the first flight of Boeing's jet-powered Dash Eighty (eventually known as the 707) in the summer of 1954 represented a far greater threat to Douglas. It was one that demanded a direct and immediate response. And that response came on June 7, 1955, when Donald Douglas formally announced his company's decision to produce a four-engine jetliner called the DC-8.

Although the DC-8 bore a close resemblance to its rival from Seattle, there were significant differences, particularly in the aerodynamics of the wing. Like the 707, the first DC-8 models were powered by Pratt & Whitney JT3C (later JT3D) engines, suspended from the wings in four pods. Passenger capacity was also similar, the main differ-

A McDonnell Douglas DC-8-62 in flight. The -62 model featured a short "stretch" over the basic DC-8 as well as a greatly increased range. (McDonnell Douglas)

An Emery Worldwide DC-8-73F freighter in a view which emphasizes its elongated, stretched fuselage. (Emery Worldwide)

ence in the two cabins being the DC-8's much larger windows. Despite its late start, Douglas made its first DC-8 sale on the same day (October 13, 1955) that Boeing sold its first 707, the two companies sharing Pan American Airway's first order for jet aircraft. Less than two weeks later, United Air Lines bought 30 DC-8s for its domestic routes. By the end of the year, Douglas had orders in hand for nearly one hundred DC-8s.

Detailed design and parts fabrication began in earnest early in 1956. A new, multi-million dollar DC-8 production plant was built at Long Beach, California. The first DC-8 began to take shape in February 1957, and the wings and fuselage were mated in October, by which time Douglas had secured 133 orders from over a dozen airlines. The roll out of the first DC-8 took place on April 9, 1958, followed by the aircraft's maiden flight on May 30. At the controls was Douglas test pilot Arnold Heimerdinger. After two hours in the air, Ship Number One touched down at Edwards Air Force Base northeast of Los Angeles.

The first eight DC-8s, including two long-range models, were used in the flight test program. While Boeing offered a choice of fuselage lengths, the early DC-8s were all

Chapter 29
Vickers VC10

Vickers' magnificent VC10 is arguably one of the most beautiful airliners ever built. Its elegant lines are surpassed only by the undeniably graceful Concorde. As a 1966 British Overseas Airways Company promotional brochure declared: "The whole appearance of this blue and white jet beauty suggests speed achieved in a lithe, graceful form—unorthodox, yet utterly obviously perfect!" However, beauty alone does not guarantee commercial success for a jetliner. And while both pilots and passengers greatly appreciated the VC10, the airplane was designed too closely around a narrow set of requirements issued by BOAC. As a result, it attracted only a handful of customers and endured a painfully short production run.

The VC10 and the longer heavier, and more powerful Super VC10 were the last airliners to bear the famous Vickers name. Although the VC10 began as a Vickers design, the firm became a part of the British Aircraft Corporation in 1960, together with the Bristol Aeroplane Company and English Electric. At the time of its first flight in 1962, the VC10 was the largest airliner ever produced in Europe and the world's most powerful jet transport. The tremendous success Vickers had enjoyed with the Viscount led to the expectation that its first pure jet would enjoy an equal measure of popularity with the airlines.

The VC10 owed its origins to the Vickers VC7 which, in turn, was a commercial development of the V.1000 military transport. Designed in response to a Royal Air Force requirement in the early 1950s, the V.1000 prototype was just months away from its first flight when the government cancelled the project in 1955. Based in part on the Vickers Valiant jet bomber, the V.1000/VC7 would have been powered by four new Rolls-Royce Conway turbofan engines buried in the wings. The VC7 could have been flying trans-Atlantic routes as early as 1959. And being similar in size to the 707 and DC-8, it could have given the big American jets some genuine competition. Sir George Edwards, BAC's Managing Director and the designer of the Viscount, described the cancellation of the V.1000/VC7 as the biggest setback in the history of the British aircraft industry. Although some of the technology would later be incorporated in the VC10, the demise of the VC7 delayed Britain's entry into the large jet market by several years and gave the American firms a huge head start.

In 1957, BOAC issued a set of requirements for a new jet transport with the same capacity as the 707 but able to serve the Corporation's Empire routes in Africa and Asia. The new airliner was also designed to replace BOAC's Britannias and Comets. Many of the intended destinations had "hot and high" airfields—airports in climates with warm ambient air (thus, "hot"), which reduces lift, and at high elevations (thus, "high"), which together with short runways compromised the 707's performance. The new transport would complement BOAC's 707s by providing a large jetliner with good short runway performance. However, management had not anticipated the fact that most runways would eventually be lengthened to accommodate other carriers' 707s and DC-8s!

On May 22, 1957, BOAC announced its intention to order the Vickers VC10. A contract was signed on January 14, 1958, for 35 airplanes with an option on 20 more. Sir George Edwards led the engineering team that designed the new jetliner. The VC10's most distinctive features were its four rear-mounted Conway engines and curved "T" tail. Less apparent to the eye were the machined skin panels. Cut from solid metal, machined skins offered increased strength and decreased weight. The VC10 was produced in Vickers' new assembly hall at Weybridge in Surrey. Before the first aircraft flew, BOAC signed another contract for ten Super VC10s, a stretched model intended for trans-Atlantic routes. The Standard VC10 could carry up to 151 passengers while the Super VC10 could seat 174 people in an all-economy configuration.

As BOAC reassessed its requirements, the VC10 order was modified a number of times. The final count was for 12 Standard and 17 Super VC10s. Unfortunately, each

This Gulf Air VC10 stopping at London's Heathrow International Airport in 1974 shows off the airliner's graceful lines. (C.F.A.P. collection)

This head-on view of a BOAC Super VC10 shows off the jetliner's clean wing, four rear-mounted engines, and T-tail in a spectacular manner. (British Airways)

change BOAC requested delayed the overall program and put Vickers further behind its rivals. In the end, the VC10's short runway capability proved unnecessary and simply made the airplane more costly to operate than later versions of the 707 and DC-8. To get the VC10 off the ground quickly, its engines gulped an inordinate amount of fuel. This, in turn, cost more money. As Sir George himself noted, "You get absolutely no medals, except from the pilots, for only using three-quarters of the runway!"

Despite these problems, the VC10 was truly an outstanding design. With Jock Bryce and Brian Trubshaw at the controls, it made its maiden flight on June 29, 1962. BOAC placed the VC10 into service on its African routes in April 1964. Because of its plush seats and comfortable cabin, the VC10 rapidly became a passenger favorite. That reputation was enhanced when the first Super VC10 entered service between London and New York a year later. BOAC news releases boasted, "This magnificent aircraft is so advanced, so luxurious, so way ahead of its time…that it has given BOAC a six-year lead over other airlines." Actually, six years later, passengers would be eagerly boarding Boeing's magnificent new 747 jumbo jets. But in 1965, BOAC could proclaim, "Flying VC10, you arrive quicker, soothed and relaxed from a flight of unparalleled serenity." This explains why BOAC's VC10 passengers remained intensely loyal to the type for the next 16 years.

Because it was so expensive to operate, the VC10 won few orders from other customers. Several African airlines used small numbers of the aircraft for routes that resembled those envisioned in BOAC's original requirements. But elsewhere, 707s, DC-8s and particularly Super DC-8s were much more economical. Only 54 VC10s were produced, 14 as military transports for the RAF. The fuel crisis of the 1970s sent most commercial VC10s into retirement. The RAF purchased most of the secondhand VC10s and converted many of them to tankers. In this new role, the beautiful VC10 still graces the skies. And while the VC10 has never won a medal for economics, it remains a beautifully designed airplane and an important milestone in the evolution of the modern airliner.

A Royal Air Force VC10 tanker in flight. The RAF is the sole remaining operator of the VC10, which it utilizes in both transport and tanker roles. (Airliners America)

Chapter 30
Sud-Aviation Caravelle

France has always been an aviation-minded nation. More than a century before the Wright Brothers, man's first flights were in the Montgolfier brothers' hot air balloons in 1783. The Brazilian-born inventor Alberto Santos-Dumont thrilled Parisians by flying around the Eiffel Tower in a dirigible of his own design in 1901. And Louis Blériot became the first man to fly across the English Channel in 1909.

The French led the way again with the first short-range production jetliner. It was called the Caravelle after the caravel merchant ships of the 15th and 16th centuries. Like those famous sailing vessels, the Jet Age Caravelle was small, light, quick, and elegant. It also pioneered the rear-engine layout that has since been used by more than a dozen other jet transports.

The Caravelle was designed to meet a government-sponsored specification for a short-haul jetliner. Several French firms were studying concepts for such an airplane as

SAS, the Scandinavian airline, was first to fly the Caravelle. (Scandinavian Airlines System)

early as 1946, but until the French government expressed official interest in 1951, none possessed the resources to actually build one. The following year, Sud–Est Aviation was authorized to develop its proposed X-210.

Sud–Est Aviation was known more formally as Société Nationale de Constructions Aéronautiques du Sud-Est. Along with Ouest-Aviation, it had been formed in 1936 by the nationalization of several private firms. Sud-Est and Ouest merged in 1957 to form Sud-Aviation, which then joined two more manufacturers to become Aérospatiale in 1970. That concern is now a world leader in the design and production of aircraft, spacecraft, rockets, and missiles and is a member of the European Airbus Industrie consortium.

The original X-210 proposal called for a trijet similar to the later Boeing 727. But in its final form, the S.E.210 emerged as a twinjet, powered by Rolls-Royce Avon engines. The rear-engine layout that had been called for in the trijet configuration was retained in the twin-engine design. With the engines mounted in pods at the rear of the fuselage, it was necessary to fix the horizontal stabilizer higher up on the tail than normal. The engine placement left the wing "clean," thus improving efficiency. Cabin noise was also reduced since the jet exhausts were located well aft of the passengers. And longitudinal stability was less affected than with wing-mounted engines since the engines were located so close to the aircraft's centerline.

The Caravelle thus introduced a configuration that was a radical departure from the design of early British and American jetliners. The triangular shape of its passenger windows was also unique. The design of the Caravelle's nose, however, was identical to the de Havilland Comet, for which the British manufacturer received a royalty. The British also provided the French with useful data regarding the Comet accidents and the hard lessons gleaned from those unforeseen tragedies.

The Caravelle went through a long development program to avoid any similar experiences. The prototype made its first flight on May 27, 1955, with senior test pilot Pierre Nadot in the left-hand seat. Also on board was flight engineer Roger Beteille, who would later become general manager of Airbus Industrie.

Air France placed the first order for a dozen Caravelles on February 3, 1956. Flight testing proceeded smoothly, but it was another three years before the type entered airline service. The Caravelle was introduced by Scandinavian Airlines System (SAS), on April 26, 1959. Air France followed ten days later. Caravelles were soon flying across Europe, the Middle East, Africa, and South America. While some people had questioned the need for a short-range pure jet, the Caravelle quickly became an extremely popular airliner. Passengers appreciated its quiet cabin and smooth ride. In fact, the Caravelle was so popular that Douglas Aircraft joined forces with Sud-Aviation to offer a turbofan version to American operators.

Douglas did not sell any Caravelles, although it would later produce its own DC-9 around a similar specification. Only one American carrier, United Air Lines, bought the

Caravelle directly from Sud-Aviation. United's 20 Caravelles were the first of the developed Series VI-R model which followed the improved Series III version, introduced by Alitalia in 1960. United ordered the more powerful VI-R that same year and started flying its first Caravelle on July 14, 1961, between New York and Chicago.

The French connection was emphasized in United's publicity campaigns. United called the airplane "La Belle Caravelle" and described it as "swift, slim, graceful...and as comfortable as she is beautiful. French-flavored decor...smooth ride...spacious accommodations...(and) incredibly quiet cabin make the Caravelle an odds-on favorite with knowledgeable travelers." United featured a 64-seat, all first-class cabin. Each airplane was named for a French city. And until the arrival of the 727 in 1964, the Caravelle gave United a distinct advantage over its propjet competitors. The airplane looked especially stylish in United's red, white, and blue livery, although the Caravelle was an undisputed beauty in almost any color and from every angle. Its curved lines truly set it apart.

With competitors coming on the scene during the mid-1960s in the form of the 727, 737, DC-9, and BAC One-Eleven, Sud-Aviation recognized the need to further

A Eureka Aviation SE-210 Caravelle. (Peter J. Sweetten/Flying Images Worldwide)

This view of an Air France Caravelle shows off the airliner's curvaceous lines. (Airliners America)

improve the Caravelle. In 1964, the first Caravelle 10B, later called the Super Caravelle, was introduced with JT8D turbofan engines and a lengthened fuselage carrying up to 104 passengers. A further stretch marked the Caravelle 12, which could accommodate 140 passengers. Production at Toulouse finally came to an end in 1972 after 282 Caravelles had been built.

Prior to the Airbus A300, which is produced at the same plant that manufactured the Caravelle, Sud-Aviation's innovative twinjet was Europe's bestselling jetliner. The Caravelle's success assured France a key role in Airbus Industrie and enabled the nation to maintain its tradition as an aviation leader.

Chapter 31
Convair 880 and 990

Production of Convair-Liners in San Diego came to an end in 1958 after some 1,075 (including military versions) of the transports had been built. Given the company's success with that program, it is not surprising that Convair decided to join Boeing and Douglas in the jetliner business. It announced its own entry, the Skylark 600 (or Model 22), in April 1956. However, Convair did not intend to compete with the long-range 707 and DC-8. Rather, its airliner, which was soon re-dubbed the "Golden Arrow," was planned to serve medium-range routes and to extend jet service to city pairs, such as Chicago and Los Angeles, and New York and Atlanta. It would also offer more comfort and greater speed than any other airliner, traveling at 600 mph, or 880 feet per second, which is how a third name for the new airliner, Convair 880, came into use later that same year.

This temporary "identity crisis" was due, in part, to the influence of Howard Hughes, who was interested in acquiring the new Convair jet for Trans World Airlines (TWA), which he owned. Hughes had begun discussing the project with the manufacturer as early as 1953, and the design that emerged was tailored in large measure to his specifica-

The first Convair 880 was painted white, with gold and black trim for its initial test flights. (Airliners America)

tions. As he had done with Lockheed and the Constellation, Hughes wanted Convair to give him a lock on the first deliveries of the Skylark so that he could beat his competitors into the air with the "World's Fastest Jetliner." To draw attention to his new airplanes, Hughes asked the company to use an anodizing process that would give their exteriors a gold finish. This feature resulted in the "Golden Arrow" name, although when it became apparent that the idea was impractical, the plan was quietly forgotten, and the new "880" name was adopted. But gold trim was eventually used throughout the 880's interior. Demanding another tailored specification, the billionaire also wanted a fuselage with a smaller diameter than the Boeing and Douglas jets; as a result, the Convair design only allowed a maximum of five seats per row. This provided more room and greater luxury, but also limited the jet's capacity to 110 passengers and raised its per seat operating cost, thus diminishing its attractiveness to airline accountants, if no one else.

When Hughes decided that TWA would only require 30 of the 40 airplanes he had been discussing with Conavir, he made ten of his delivery options available to Delta Air Lines. The two carriers announced their orders in June 1956, officially launching the program. To break into the market, Convair sold these first aircraft for less than their actual cost. This was just one more in a growing series of poor decisions that had begun with Hughes' involvement in the project—his seemingly endless design changes had already seriously compromised the 880's future.

The first 880 took off from San Diego on its maiden flight on January 27, 1959. It looked regal in its white and gold color scheme, and flight testing went smoothly. The transport was equipped with General Electric CJ-805 turbojet engines, a civil version of the military J79 which powered Convair's supersonic B-58 bomber. The first 880 deliveries to TWA were planned for November of that year.

Unfortunately, despite his wealth, Howard Hughes had failed to put together a workable plan to finance his 880 order, and it soon became apparent that TWA would be unable to accept the airplanes as scheduled. Moreover, only a handful of additional 880 orders had trickled in, leaving Convair without any additional customers to take the jets. The first two TWA 880s were towed from the factory to a nearby hangar and placed under guard. Eighteen others were pulled off the production line in various stages of completion and left in open storage beneath the southern California sun.

Meanwhile, Delta Air Lines took delivery of its first aircraft in February 1960, and inaugurated 880 service on May 15 between New York and New Orleans. Delta's jets were finished in an elegant all-white finish with 76 first class seats plus 12 more seats in a forward lounge (or "club compartment" as the airline called it). The new 880s were an immediate hit with passengers and crews alike, and the type maintained its popularity throughout its lifetime.

TWA's problems were finally resolved, and the airline put its first 880s into service on January 12, 1961. But the delay had cost Convair a fortune, as each of the TWA

The Convair 990 had a striking appearance with its rakish lines and distinctive "speed pods" atop its wings. (American Airlines)

airplanes had to be hand-finished outdoors. TWA eventually acquired a total of 27 880s, while Delta's fleet grew to 17. Additional orders came from several overseas customers for a longer range model called the 880M. When Convair ended 880 production in 1962, a mere 65 aircraft had been built, while a staggering $450 million had been lost, the largest single financial loss in US corporate history up to the time.

The 880's sales potential had been undermined by Boeing's 720, a high-speed, medium-range adaptation of the 707. But throwing good money after bad, Convair focused on its own adaptation: a bigger faster longer range version of the 880, called the 990 (or Model 30 or Coronado, as it was known overseas). The 990 was designed to meet an American Airlines requirement and that carrier launched the program with an order for 25 airliners in July 1958. The airplane would be ten feet longer than the 880 in order to accommodate up to 121 passengers, and new GE CJ-805-23B turbofan engines would push it along at 635 mph.

During a test flight in 1961, a 990 reached Mach 0.97 or 675 mph. To achieve such high speeds, drag was reduced by mounting four distinctive "speed pods" on top of the wings, which were also used to carry fuel.

The first 990 flight took place on January 24, 1961, and it quickly became apparent that the type's performance was below the guarantees made to American Airlines. Through a series of costly modifications, Convair rectified the jet's assorted problems. Swissair inaugurated Coronado flights on March 9, 1962, followed nine days later by American. Within a few short years, the US airline started selling the fuel-thirsty jets to secondhand operators, although the model had been extremely popular with passengers.

In the end, only 37 of the 990 model were produced. With the fuel crisis in the 1970s, speed was no longer paramount, and the 880 and 990 both became too costly for most carriers to operate. The graceful jets went into early retirement. They were the last airliners that Convair would ever build.

A Garuda Indonesian Airways Convair 990 receives ground service. (C.F.A.P. collection)

Chapter 32
D.H.121 Trident

Hundreds of airliners have been designed and built over the years, but only a relative handful were sold in great enough numbers to be commercially successful, thus earning the manufacturers a worthwhile return on their investments. Those which failed did so for a variety of reasons: the Douglas DC–4E was too big; the Avro Canada Jetliner was too early; the Bristol Brabazon was too slow; and the de Havilland Trident, our current subject, was too small.

The Trident's story is particularly painful because the original design was closer in size than the final version to the highly successful Boeing 727. Indeed, the two airplanes looked very much alike and were intended for the same market. Yet, in the end, the 727 accounted for over 90 percent of their combined sales. The difference was the result of the British trijet being tailored too closely to the individual specifications of a single customer. It was the same mistake that Vickers had made with the VC10, both projects

This view of the first Trident reveals the airliner's unique offset nose gear and the unusual four-wheel single axle main landing gear. (British Aerospace)

A C.A.A.C. D.H. Trident making a landing. The Trident was the British response to the French Caravelle. (Airliners America)

having been more influenced by domestic British political concerns than the needs of the world market.

The Trident was a response, in part, to the French-built Caravelle. Not long after Air France ordered the twinjet, British European Airways (BEA) issued its requirement for a jetliner that could carry 100 passengers at 600 mph over 1,000 miles from existing runways. By the spring of 1957, Avro, Bristol, and de Havilland were each presenting their design proposals to BEA. After reviewing them all, the government-owned airline favored de Havilland's D.H. 121.

The new transport featured three tail-mounted engines—two in pods on either side of the fuselage, and the third centered inside the rear of the airframe. A large intake at the base of the T-tail fed air to the middle engine through an S-shaped duct. De Havilland engineers believed three powerplants would be more cost-effective than four, and safer than two. Their design also included swept back wings, a relatively wide cabin permitting six-abreast (three seats on each side of a single aisle) seating in economy class, a provision for built-in forward airstairs, and an unusual set of landing gear. This was comprised of nose gear, which was offset from the aircraft's centerline so that it would retract sideways into the fuselage, thus making room for a large underfloor equipment bay housing avionics and electrical systems. The main landing gear was also unique in that its tires were aligned along a single axis. For stowage, each four-wheel gear had to be twisted through 90 degrees before retraction.

One more interesting feature was designed into the D.H.121 from the outset: an automatic flight control and landing system which would eventually permit "hands off" landings. The system was designed to increase safety and regularity, enabling the Trident to "see" its way electronically (and automatically) all the way from mid-flight to touchdown, even in foul weather and near-zero visibility. Like its famous predecessor, the de Havilland Comet, this second generation jetliner was introducing some innovative engineering concepts.

De Havilland received a letter of intent from BEA for 24 D.H.121s in February 1958, thus giving the company the impetus to start detailed design work. Unfortunately, at this point, much of the Trident's future sales potential was compromised because the airline called for a somewhat smaller aircraft than originally planned for. The result was a reduction in fuselage length (though not width), a smaller wing area, and substitution of the less powerful Rolls-Royce RB163 Spey engines for the original RB141 Medways. While this modified design made BEA happy, it gave Boeing's bigger 727 the performance edge in later years.

A formal contract for 24 aircraft (with 12 options) was signed in August 1959. De Havilland promised to deliver the first Trident by 1963. In 1960, the company was brought into the Hawker Siddeley Group (explaining why the jetliner was also known as the Hawker Siddeley Trident). The first flight took off from de Havilland's runway at Hatfield on January 9, 1962, with veteran test pilot John Cunningham, who had also flown the first Comet, at the controls. Two years of testing culminated in the first delivery to BEA in December 1963, with scheduled service over BEA's European routes starting on April 1, 1964. Although Boeing had launched the 727 program after the Trident, it beat its British rival into airline service by 60 days.

The first production model of the D.H.121 was called the Trident 1C. Although it met BEA's performance specifications, Hawker Siddeley recognized that other carriers would need a more capable model. In August 1962, Kuwait Airways placed a small order for the Trident 1E which included, among other improvements, an extended wing, an extra fuel tank, and uprated engines, all of which contributed to improved performance. Several other airlines in Europe, Asia, and the Middle East also ordered the 1E. The Trident 2E was a longer range model introduced by BEA in 1968 (the carrier called it the "Trident Two"). A stretched version, the Trident 3B, entered service with BEA in 1971. It was 16 feet longer than its predecessors, and carried up to 140 passengers in economy class (180 in a high-density layout). A small booster engine was mounted above the center engine to provide increased thrust during takeoff and climb.

Over half of the 117 Tridents produced were flown by BEA, which became a part of British Airways in 1973. The only other substantial orders came from China, which bought 33 Trident 2Es and 2 Super 3Bs (a long-range Trident 3B). The BEA aircraft remained a familiar sight at European airports for more than two decades, with the last British Airways flight taking place on December 31, 1985.

While Boeing won the vast majority of early trijet sales with its 727, the Trident did earn a noteworthy distinction on March 5, 1964, when it became the first airliner to make a fully automatic landing during a test flight at Bedford. On June 10, 1965, BEA made the first automatic touchdown while carrying passengers in scheduled service using the "Autoland" system which had been developed by Hawker Siddeley and Smith Industries for the D.H.121. Thus, while the Trident was a disappointment commercially, it was a genuine technological pioneer.

This rear view of the Trident displays its three rear-mounted engines and the S-duct which feeds air to the center engine embedded in the airliner's airframe. (C.F.A.P. collection)

Chapter 33
Boeing 727

By 1960, long-distance passengers were being introduced to the Jet Age on board Boeing 707s, Douglas DC-8s, and, in smaller numbers, Comet 4s. In Europe, short-haul travelers were enjoying the Caravelle. But the bulk of the world's air routes were still being served by propeller-driven aircraft, including large numbers of piston-powered airliners such as the DC-6 and Constellation. The popularity of the early jetliners on long-haul flights rapidly created a demand for pure jets on shorter trips. While a 707 offered little advantage over an Electra on a flight between Chicago and Washington, D.C. (the difference in the scheduled arrival and departure times amounting to less than half an hour), people were far more impressed by the 707. At the beginning of the Jet Age, everyone wanted to fly on a jet. This, of course, is still the case today.

As the 1960s began, the Caravelle had enough range to provide short-haul service between major European cities. For especially busy routes, Britain was developing the

An American Airlines 727-100 climbs away after takeoff. This original, short-bodied model had a cabin divided by a galley located just ahead of the wing. (American Airlines)

de Havilland Trident, a three-engine jetliner seating up to 103 passengers. But American carriers needed an airplane with greater range and payload as well as a jet transport with short field capability. The runways at some of America's busiest and most important airports—Chicago's Midway, New York's La Guardia and Washington's National—were too short to accommodate early jetliners. An exception was the Avro Canada Jetliner, which had been cancelled before entering service a decade earlier.

Boeing engineers had been studying various concepts for a medium-range jet transport when the 707 entered service. While the 720 represented an interim solution in terms of range and payload, it was not the short field contender the carriers desired. Under Jack Steiner's design leadership, the 727 emerged as a response to the airlines' short field requirements. When Boeing announced the first 727 sales to United Airlines and Eastern Airlines on December 5, 1960, the firm was offering what looked like a slightly enlarged Trident. Indeed, the 727 adopted the same three-engine layout as the Trident, although Boeing opted for the more powerful Pratt & Whitney JT8D powerplant. The American jet also incorporated more advanced high-lift flaps which, together with added thrust, gave the 727 better short field performance than its British counterpart. Like the Trident, the 727 utilized a unique "T" tail.

De Havilland's original proposal for the Trident was very similar to the later 727. But like so many other British transports, the Trident was tailored too closely to the home market. British European Airways asked the firm to scale down its original design, and as a result, only 117 Tridents were built. This compared to an eventual total of 1,832 727s sold, making the Boeing product one of the bestselling airliners ever. Had the Seattle company focused on the specific requirements of any one of its original 727 customers, a very different design would likely have emerged. By looking for some common denominators, Boeing produced an incredibly successful design.

The company also looked for commonality. Although the 727 was its first trimotored aircraft since the Model 80 three decades earlier, it shared many design features with the 707 and 720. The most obvious was the nose section, but the upper fuselage was also identical, giving the 727 the same cabin size and furnishings as its four-engine predecessors and greatly reducing manufacturing costs by sharing some common tooling. A few years later, the design of the 737 twinjet would again adopt this practice. Airlines were thus offered the opportunity to build their fleets around a family of Boeing jetliners with widely differing capabilities but utilizing many of the same parts and systems. Repair and maintenance were simplified accordingly.

Lew Wallick and Dix Loesch took the 727 up for its maiden flight on February 9, 1963. It was certified by the end of that year and entered service with Eastern Air Lines on February 1, 1964. United Air Lines followed five days later. Lufthansa was the first overseas customer, putting the 727 into service between Dusseldorf and London in April. The airliner was soon flying with American, TWA, National, Northwest, and Pan American. The Jet Age had arrived on most major air routes, including short-haul runs.

Oddly enough, the 727 did not have any real competition. The market was wide open!

A promotional brochure issued by United at the time of the 727's introduction emphasized safety. "Three rugged engines of proven design…three separate hydraulic flight control systems…and three skilled pilots back the 727's dependability," it proclaimed. The brochure described the short field capabilities and "spectacular" performance of United's "revolutionary" new short- to medium-range 727 Jet Mainliner.

Unfortunately, the 727's early career was marred by some fatal accidents. United lost an airplane over Lake Michigan on August 16, 1965. Less than three months later, two 727s crashed on landing within three days of each other, both with heavy loss of life. A few pilots were evidently having difficulty making the transition from old propeller aircraft to the high-performance 727. These problems were corrected, and investigation revealed no fault with the 727's design. Soon hundreds of 727s being built at Boeing's Renton plant were giving yeoman service around the globe.

This United 727-200 rests on the tarmac at Chicago's O'Hare Field in 1977. In addition to a longer fuselage, the center engine intake on the 727-200 was circular, not round as on the 727-100.
(Bill Mellberg)

The Boeing 727 became a workhorse of the world's airlines during the 1970s. (Boeing)

The outstanding success of the basic 727 inevitably led to a stretched version, the 727-200. Making its first flight on July 27, 1967, the new model featured among many improvements a 20-foot increase in length, which enabled the airplane to carry up to 189 passengers. It went into service with Northeast Airlines in December. The longer-range Advanced 727-200 was introduced in 1970. Two different freighter versions of the 727 were also offered.

By the time production ended in 1984, the 727 had become in many respects the world's standard jetliner. It was efficient on both busy shuttle corridors and medium-range international routes. The 727 not only replaced propeller airliners, but also greatly contributed to the tremendous growth in air travel during the 1960s, 1970s and 1980s. The trijet secured Boeing's position as the undisputed world leader in commercial aircraft design and manufacturing and is, for many, the Jet Age equivalent of the Douglas DC-3. Which is, perhaps, as fine a tribute as any that can be paid to one of aviation's most important airliners.

Chapter 34
NAMC YS-11

Japanese industry is the source of a wide range of products, from cars and motor-cycles to cameras and stereo equipment. Marketing expertise and close attention to quality control have earned Japan an enviable record of success in the worldwide sales of its consumer goods. Although the country exports many different industrial goods, from microchips to giant ships, it has never been known for producing commercial airliners. There is one exception: the NAMC YS-11.

Although production of the NAMC YS-11 ended in 1973 after only 182 had been built, the YS-11 made its mark on the airline industry and many models remain in use today. It was, in some respects, ahead of its time, offering up to 64 seats on commuter routes when most aircraft in its class accommodated 50 or fewer passengers. However, because the YS-11's operating costs were similar to its smaller competitors, it could earn more for its operators on any given flight simply by carrying more people. The newest

Piedmont Airlines bought 21 YS-11As for its short-haul routes in the southeastern United States. The regional carrier, which later merged with USAir, operated YS-11s from 1968 through 1982. (Piedmont Airlines)

regional airliners now provide the same seating capacity that the YS-11 was offering over 30 years ago.

But the story of the YS-11 goes back much farther than that. It begins in early postwar Japan when, after their wartime aircraft industry had been destroyed, the country's leaders began to consider how it might be redeveloped. Reconstruction was allowed under the Peace Treaty of 1952.

Initially, a few of the better-known wartime aircraft manufacturers such as Mitsubishi, Showa, Kawasaki, Kawanishi (reformed as Shin Meiwa), and Nakajima (reformed as Fuji) began overhauling US military aircraft based in Japan. Later, some of these firms started manufacturing American airplanes under licensing agreements, a practice that continues today. But prior to and during the war, these companies had designed and built their own airplanes. In fact, they built some of the finest military aircraft flown during World War II. Kawanishi was best known for its big seaplanes and flying boats. Kawasaki had built high-speed fighters, and Mitsubishi produced G4M "Betty" bombers as well as the legendary A6M Zero fighters. Between 1920 and 1945, Mitsubishi turned out some 80,000 airplanes of nearly 100 different models!

But one type of aircraft that Japanese industry had never produced on its own was a commercial airliner. Showa had manufactured DC-3s under license before the war. Kawasaki built a number of Lockheed 14s under a similar arrangement. And Nakajima had produced it own small twin-engine transport known as the Ki-34, but it only carried eight passengers and was mostly used in military roles.

In the postwar environment, however, Japanese authorities turned their attention to the commercial market, including commercial aviation. Given their lack of experience in producing large transport aircraft, a medium-sized airliner seemed to be the most reasonable undertaking. With that goal in mind, the government decided to subsidize such a project beginning in 1957. Work on the design had begun the previous year at the urging of the Ministry of International Trade and Industry.

Detailed studies were carried out under the leadership of Dr. Hidemasa Kimura, and the Transport Aircraft Development Association (TADA) was formed to provide overall management of the program. Six different Japanese firms combined their resources to develop the airliner, including Mitsubishi, Kawasaki, Fuji, Shin Meiwa, Showa, and Nihon Hikoki. If some of these names sound familiar, it is because they belong to huge industrial enterprises that manufacture a variety of products that are used throughout the world.

In 1959, following the amendment of the Aircraft Industries Promotion Law, TADA was succeeded by Nihon Aeroplane Manufacturing Company (NAMC). Pooling private and government funds, NAMC was given the overall responsibility to produce what, by then, was known as the YS-11. NAMC did not have its own production facilities, so the work was divided among the six partners. Kawasaki built the wings, Fuji built the tails, and so forth. Mitsubishi provided the fuselages as well as the final assembly line.

This YS-11 is flown by the Geological Survey of Japan. (Airliners America)

To power the YS-11, NAMC chose a modified version of the world's most proven and reliable turboprop engine—the Rolls-Royce Dart—the engine which also powered its competitors. The YS-11 prototype first took to the air from Nagoya on August 30, 1962, and the flight test program proceeded smoothly, with Japanese type certification being granted on August 25, 1964. The first commercial service with the YS-11 was inaugurated in April 1965 by Toa Airways, a Japanese carrier. Other Japanese airlines soon followed.

But export sales, which were the main motivation for the airliner's development, were not quick in coming. Thus NAMC introduced the new YS-11A, which offered improved performance and made the YS-11 more attractive to overseas customers. One of the first was Piedmont Airlines, which ordered ten YS-11As in 1967. By 1968, the American regional carrier had put 21 of the airliners into service. Although it proved to be popular with passengers and pilots alike, there was an interesting problem at first, stemming from what one Piedmont executive described as "the inherent difference between American and Japanese posteriors." American airline executives thought the seats were too small and too hard to appeal to American travelers. NAMC replaced them with larger softer models, and the YS-11 went on to earn a reputation for reliability—and comfort.

Piedmont retired the last of its YS-11s in 1982. But the type had been sold to many other airlines around the world, and was soon doing well on the used airplane market. It is still in service with a number of carriers, including Airborne Express, which flies 11 ex-Piedmont YS-11As as freighters (a large cargo door having been installed at the rear of its airplanes).

Although it was not a great commercial success, and NAMC was disbanded after the last airplane was built, the YS-11 did succeed in giving Japan some valuable experience in producing and supporting a commercial transport. The YS-11 was Japan's first airliner…but probably not it's last!

The prototype YS-11 first flew on August 30, 1962. Service was inaugurated in April 1965 by Toa Airways of Japan. The aircraft shown here is flown by Japan Trans Ocean Air. (Peter J. Sweetten/ Flying Images Worldwide)

Chapter 35
BAC One-Eleven

The introduction of modern jetliners followed a logical progression from long-range routes, for which the increased speed of jets made the most economic sense, to medium-range routes, which carried the largest proportion of air travelers, to short-haul intercity routes. This last step was the most challenging as propjets were considerably more economical to operate than pure jets between short distance city pairs such as Chicago and Peoria. Yet both manufacturers and air carriers recognized that once the "turbine revolution" had begun, passengers would demand pure jet service at every level of air travel. Today, even commuter and regional airlines are able to offer pure jets with the Canadair Regional Jet. But in the early 1960s, a growing need developed for a jetliner to replace Convairs, Martins—and even Viscounts—on short-haul flights scheduled by the major carriers to feed their long-distance routes.

Designing short-haul jet transports presents a number of special problems to engineers. In comparison to medium- and long-range aircraft, they make more flights, re-

Braniff International was one of the first airlines to put the BAC One-Eleven into short-haul service. (Braniff Airways)

peatedly subjecting their structures to the loads accompanying takeoff, climb, descent, and landing. The airframes of short-haul aircraft thus need to be fabricated to withstand these repeated stresses. Short-haul airliners must also provide quick "turnarounds"—the time required between landing and takeoff at each point along a multi-stop, "milk run" route must be as brief as possible. A good short-haul design will therefore accommodate rapid passenger and baggage loading and unloading. Finally, if the aircraft can be engineered to be independent of ground equipment such as air-conditioning and power units during turnarounds, considerable time can be saved.

These represented substantial challenges at a time when Boeing 707s and DC-8s required many different power carts, service units, and loading stairs at each and every stopover. To be profitable, a short-haul jet would need to be far more self-sufficient. With a large market at stake, engineers on both sides of the Atlantic were working hard to find the right combination of solutions to these challenges.

The British had been the first to introduce both jets and propjets into airline service. It is therefore not surprising that British engineers were the first to tackle a design for a short-haul jetliner. As early as 1956, Hunting Aircraft Ltd. had studied concepts for a small jet transport. The H.107, as the project was called, would offer "jet appeal" to short-haul passengers and could serve as an eventual Viscount replacement. The Hunting designers believed that the configuration adopted by Sud-Est for the Caravelle offered many advantages which they incorporated into the H.107. These included rear-mounted twin engines and a clean wing, which permitted good field performance and easy ground access to baggage holds and service ports. Integral airstairs in the tail, together with optional forward airsteps, allowed simultaneous loading and unloading of passengers during short stopovers. The H.107 was designed to carry up to 55 passengers in a relatively wide cabin which permitted five-abreast seating.

Hunting Aircraft became a part of the British Aircraft Corporation in 1960. BAC decided early on to continue the H.107 project but to enlarge the design to seat up to 74 passengers. The Rolls-Royce Spey turbofan was selected as the powerplant, and a new name, BAC One-Eleven, was adopted for the revised aircraft. The company made a final decision to launch the One-Eleven in April 1961. The first order was received in May when British United Airways bought ten airplanes. Braniff International followed with an order for six in October. Other carriers signing contracts for the new short-haul jet included Mohawk Airlines and American Airlines. This early commitment to the type by three American carriers was viewed by BAC as an especially promising development. American Airlines' order was the first for the heavier longer-range Series 400 model.

The One-Eleven's maiden flight took place on August 20, 1963, by which time about 60 aircraft had been ordered. Unfortunately, the flight test program was marred by the fatal crash of the first aircraft two months later. The cause was identified as a "deep stall" resulting from the effects of the new T-tail configuration. Consequently, the One-

American Airlines flew the largest BAC One-Eleven fleet. The Series 400 models were aptly dubbed "400 Astrojets" by American. (American Airlines)

Eleven, as well as all subsequent T-tail aircraft, was equipped with stall warning devices to prevent similar situations from occurring.

British United Airways inaugurated One-Eleven service with the Series 200 model on April 9, 1965. Mohawk followed soon after. The airplane was well received by air travelers and brought the Jet Age for the first time to cities such as Brownsville, Fort Smith, Lubbock, and Sioux Falls. Braniff touted the One-Eleven's ability to "offer full jet service to passengers on even the shortest trips."

According to Mohawk Airlines' 1965 annual report, its One-Elevens increased passenger boardings almost immediately by an average of 35 percent where the jets replaced piston equipment on the Mohawk flight schedule. Serving smaller cities in the northeastern United States, Mohawk was so pleased with the public response to the One-Eleven that it ordered additional aircraft less than a year after receiving its first One-Eleven. The airline received five One-Elevens during 1965 and encountered few problems with integrating them into its system. As the report noted: "It was immediately evident that the built-in ground capabilities of the One-Eleven…would greatly reduce required turnaround time. Mohawk's (fully loaded) One-Elevens…are turned around at terminal points in ten minutes and serviced at intermediate points with partial passenger loads on and off, including fuel, in six [minutes]."

The success of the One-Eleven generated demand for a larger model. With a 13½-foot fuselage stretch and extended wingtips, the Series 500 increased seating to 99 passengers. This version first flew on June 30, 1967, and entered service with British European Airways in 1968.

Altogether, BAC—which became a part of British Aerospace in 1977—produced 235 One-Elevens in five different series. Kits for 21 additional aircraft were supplied to Romania where the "Rombac" One-Eleven was built under license. Only nine of those airplanes were completed, although several attempts have been made to resurrect the project. In all, the BAC One-Eleven enjoyed a modest measure of success as the world's first genuine short-haul jet transport. More importantly, it set the first standard for short-haul jet transport, an example that was not lost on the world's other leading aircraft manufacturers.

A British Airways BAC One-Eleven Series 500 cruises by, its rear-mounted jets all but hidden. (Airliners America)

Chapter 36
Douglas DC-9

During the height of World War II, a few visionaries in Congress saw a future need for local airline service to small- and medium-sized American communities. Between 1946 and 1950, some 200 cities were authorized to receive local air transportation, and a group of fledgling local airlines was certified by the Civil Aeronautics Board to provide that service. Among these new carriers were such names as Allegheny, Mohawk, Piedmont, Lake Central, Ozark, Trans-Texas, North Central, Frontier, Southern, and Pacific. All of these airlines are gone now, with most having been incorporated into larger systems. A few grew into national carriers and were in turn replaced on local routes by today's regional airlines. But when the original local service airlines got their start flying secondhand DC-3s, few people imagined that airports would eventually replace train stations in places such as Green Bay, Poughkeepsie, Kalamazoo, and Champaign-Urbana.

Railroads had traditionally provided links between small towns and major cities. But as the airline industry grew during the 1950s and airliners slowly began to take over

The DC-9 boasted five-abreast seating, a ventral stairway in the tail, and integral airstairs in the front of the airliner. (C.F.A.P. collection)

Ozark Air Lines was one of the first "local service" carriers to receive the DC-9 in 1966. Here one of the original short-bodied Series 10 models makes its way across the sky. (Ozark Air Lines)

local and regional transport from railroads, a demand developed for bigger and faster airplanes on local service routes. Convairs and Martinliners replaced DC-3s, and a few carriers even ordered new turboprop airplanes such as the Fairchild F 27. By the mid-1960s, airlines were carrying most medium- and long-distance travelers. This rapid growth was largely the result of the popularity of the new jetliners. It was only natural, therefore, that local service carriers—and their passengers—wanted to bring the Jet Age to "Main Street, USA."

Douglas Aircraft Company, like other manufacturers, had foreseen this demand and was working on concepts for a short- to medium-range jetliner as early as 1959. The original DC-9 was, in essence, a scaled-down DC-8. But as Douglas engineers continued their discussions with airline executives, a new twin-engine design emerged. By the time the company launched the DC-9 program in April 1963, the airplane looked very similar to the BAC One-Eleven, which now had a two-year lead in the marketplace.

Nevertheless, Delta Air Lines placed its first order for 15 DC-9s the next month, and other carriers soon followed. The original Series 10 aircraft could seat 80 passengers, five abreast, and was able to utilize the short runways at existing airfields (which could not accommodate larger jets), and could economically fly routes ranging from 100 to 1,500 miles. Among the first customers were international carriers such as Air Canada, Swissair, and TWA, as well as local service airlines such as Bonanza and West Coast.

The first flight took place on February 25, 1965. By that time, Douglas had already received orders and options for some 250 airplanes, which was greater than the final production total for the competing BAC One-Eleven. Five aircraft were used in an intensive flight test program which resulted in the DC-9 receiving its type FAA approval in November 1965. The world's first DC-9 service was flown by Delta from Atlanta to Memphis to Kansas City on December 8, 1965. More significant were the deliveries to local carriers such as Ozark Air Lines, which initiated DC-9 service the following sum-

Here an example of the stretched, enhanced MD-80, which was based on the design of the DC-9, is seen in flight. (Crossair)

mer to smaller cities such as Peoria, Sioux City, Springfield, and Waterloo from Chicago and St. Louis. Following the BAC One-Eleven's lead, the DC-9 had succeeded in bringing the Jet Age to Main Street.

Larger carriers, such as Eastern Air Lines, also had a requirement for a short-haul jet but needed greater passenger capacity. So Douglas launched the Series 30, the first stretched DC-9. The Series 20 had consisted of ten "hot-rod" models for Scandinavian Airlines System; these utilized the Series 10 fuselage but came equipped with the longer wing, leading edge slats, and more powerful engines of the Series 30 (which improved the takeoff performance of this model at "hot and high" airfields). The DC-9-30 was nearly 15 feet longer than the DC-9-10, and could carry up to 105 passengers. Eastern ordered this version in 1965. The first flight took place on August 1, 1966, with service initiated the following year. The extended wings and full-length slats which had been introduced on the Series 20 resulted in improved DC-9-30 performance. By the time the first Series 30 flew, overall DC-9 sales had grown to 375 aircraft. For the next ten years, the DC-9 order book continued to grow. Douglas introduced three new stretched versions, each longer than the last — the Series 40, Series 50, and Series 80. The Series 50 carried 125 passengers, and the Series 80 (or "Super 80") had 155 seats. By this time, 976 DC-9s had been built and sold.

In 1977, McDonnell Douglas — the two airplane builders having merged a decade earlier — announced the MD-80 series of "high-tech" jetliners based on the proven design of the DC-9. These represented a further evolution of the Series 80 with enough improvements to merit a new name and branch on the family tree. The first MD-80 flew on October 18, 1979. It was more than 40 feet longer than the DC-9 Series 10 and lifted twice the payload. The MD-87 was a shorter version with increased range. On February 22, 1993, the re-engined MD-90 took off on its maiden flight. Another five-foot fuselage stretch enabled the MD-90 to seat 172 passengers — more than twice as many as the original DC-9! The MD-90 is 152.6 feet long and has a 107.8-foot wingspan. Its range is 2,610 statute miles. What started out as a short-haul local-service jetliner has evolved into a transcontinental twinjet, carrying as many travelers as the early four-engine DC-8s.

Over 30 years after the first DC-9 took off from the Douglas plant at Long Beach, California, that airplane's successors are still rolling down the assembly line. Over 2,300 Douglas twinjets have been sold. And by virtue of its fuel efficiency, advanced systems and quiet V2500 engines, the MD-90 represents "technology for the 21st Century," as a McDonnell Douglas brochure describes it. But the August 1997 merger of McDonnell Douglas with Boeing marked the end of the line for Douglas-designed airliners.

Meanwhile, the original DC-9 is still in service around the globe and most likely will remain in use for years to come. Like the Douglas DC-3, its famous twin-engine ancestor, the dependable DC-9 has truly become a classic in its own time.

Chapter 37
Boeing 737

When Boeing announced its decision to produce a short-haul jet on February 22, 1965, very few people could have imagined that it was destined to become the world's bestselling airliner. After all, the Boeing 737 was the last entry in the marketplace. Boeing's announcement came just as the BAC One-Eleven was about to enter service, and only three days before the first flight of the Douglas DC-9. The company's competitors had a considerable lead. But being last can have its advantages. And for those customers willing or able to wait for it, the 737 offered some definite advantages.

Foremost among them was "commonality"—the feature that made the 727 so attractive to both airlines and passengers. Indeed, while the little 737 incorporated many of the lessons and design approaches that Boeing developed for the big, four-engine 707, it had even more in common with the company's highly successful trijet. Both airplanes

This view of a Delta Air Lines 737-200 demonstrates how closely the engines are tucked under the airliner's wings. (Delta Air Lines)

Like other jets designed for short-haul routes, the 737 featured a self-contained airstairs which facilitated fast turnarounds at intermediate stops. The early model 737s looked a bit chubby because their short fuselages housed wide six-abreast cabins. (United Airlines)

were powered by Pratt & Whitney JT8D engines, and an astounding 60 percent of the 737's parts were shared with the 727. These included not only cabin furnishings from the 727, but more expensive components—for example, doors, windows, panels, ceilings, and the basic fuselage structures—were also interchangeable. And if you were viewing only the nose section, it was difficult to distinguish a 737 from a 727—or a 707.

Like the 727, the 737 was essentially the same in terms of comfort as a 707 Intercontinental. Business travelers could thus enjoy the same spacious seating while flying between Chicago and Grand Rapids that they had come to expect on 727s between Chicago and New York, or on 707s on trans-Atlantic or transcontinental flights. The big jets had set the standard for comfort in air travel, and in designing the 737, Boeing had decided to produce the only short-haul jetliner that would fully adhere to that standard.

of the older models. These latest versions will incorporate numerous improvements, including changes in materials, systems, and instrumentation, thus keeping the 737 at technology's leading edge.

By 1998, more than 4,100 737s had been sold, making it the world's bestselling jetliner by a wide margin. Boeing's 737 order book continues to grow with deliveries now scheduled well beyond the year 2000. But apart from its record sales, the 737 has earned an even greater distinction. It has given birth to countless new airlines and contributed to the spectacular growth of world air traffic. At any given moment, more than 800 737s are in the air, carrying passengers to every corner of the globe. The 737 is, indeed, aviation's "Little Giant."

Chapter 38
de Havilland Canada DHC-6 Twin Otter

If the legendary DC-3 can be said to have given birth to the mainstream airline business, then in many respects a small and frequently overlooked Canadian-built airplane, the de Havilland Canada DHC-6 Twin Otter, can be said to have given birth to modern short-haul transport. Rugged and versatile, Twin Otters are at home in every environment imaginable, from equatorial jungles to Alpine ski resorts. The DHC-6 has brought civilization to some of the world's most primitive cultures and a whole new level of air service to some of its most advanced societies. It has saved many lives and made a few fortunes. It has been used by airlines, scientific expeditions, military forces, police forces, missionaries, and industrial giants in a variety of roles almost too numerous to count. In short, while it is often taken for granted, the Twin Otter is truly one of history's most significant air transports.

The Twin Otter's short takeoff and landing—known as "STOL"—capability enables it to use short runways inaccessible to other airliners, making it an ideal backwoods transport, as well as a successful small city airport aircraft. (Mike Beedell)

The Twin Otter—like the DC-3—can fill many roles. This one serves with the Royal Canadian Mounted Police. (Royal Canadian Mounted Police)

The Twin Otter's story begins in England with Sir Geoffrey de Havilland, whose career encompassed an era extending from the earliest biplanes to the de Havilland Comet, the world's first jet airliner. In 1928, Sir Geoffrey founded a Canadian subsidiary, de Havilland Aircraft of Canada Ltd. — or DHC — to assemble and sell the de Havilland D.H.60 Moth. A small, two-seat biplane, the Moth made flying both affordable and accessible. It was followed by a series of derivatives, including the D.H.82 Tiger Moth, one of the most popular training aircraft ever built. The Tiger Moth was also the first airplane fully manufactured by DHC. Over a thousand of them were built during World War II at the company's Downsview plant near Toronto, along with several hundred Avro Ansons, and more than a thousand D.H.98 Mosquitos.

Having enlarged its production capacity and engineering expertise during the war years, DHC created its first indigenous design, the DHC-1 Chipmunk all-metal trainer, in 1946. The following year, the company produced its DHC-2 Beaver, which was a rugged and popular bush plane. Some 1,700 Beavers were sold around the world, with many still providing reliable daily service. Much of the Beaver's great success was attrib-

Colombia's ACES was one of many airlines to order the DHC-6 Twin Otter for commuter and "feeder" routes. Here a new Twin Otter has just been rolled out of the DHC factory at Downsview.
(de Havilland Canada)

utable to its short takeoff and landing (or "STOL") capabilities. STOL enabled the Beaver to use floats and skis as readily as wheels. Beavers could be equipped, in effect, as flying canoes and dog-sleds, and were especially well-suited to Canada's vast interior as well as to other remote locales around the globe.

In response to a call from both military and civilian operators for a larger STOL aircraft, de Havilland produced the DHC-3 Otter in 1950, with twice the payload of the Beaver. The company sold 466 Otters and then moved on to the DHC-4 Caribou and DHC-5 Buffalo, both military STOL transports. In 1963, DHC began work on a new improved twin-engine version of the single-engine Otter. This DHC-6 Twin Otter differed from the DHC-3 in several respects. The fuselage was lengthened, the tail was redesigned, and a tricycle landing gear was incorporated. But the greatest difference was the use of two Pratt & Whitney PT6A turboprop engines, which provided exceptional performance. On May 20, 1965, the Twin Otter prototype made its maiden flight from Downsview, and in 1966, the first production aircraft was delivered to the Ontario Department of Lands and Forests.

The Twin Otter design had been based on the requirements of the US Army which, in the end, never placed an order for the type. But in losing a customer, DHC gained a market, for the capabilities of the Twin Otter helped to spawn a whole new breed of airline. This became apparent after the new Twin Otter was demonstrated in 1966 in the United States at the Reading Air Show. Among those who admired its size and STOL performance were the presidents of several "air taxi" operators, small carriers which were forerunners of commuter and regional airlines. Flying small aircraft with fewer than ten seats, they served short low-traffic routes. Most passengers were business people in a hurry. Like the rest of the airline industry at the time, the commuter carriers were regulated by the US government. The Twin Otter met all US regulations while seating up to 18 (later 20) passengers. Moreover, it was inexpensive both to purchase and operate. Within a very short time, the Twin Otter was a familiar sight at small airports across the United States and Canada and around the world. Its economics enabled the air taxi operators of the 1960s to grow into the commuter airlines of the 1970s.

While the "STOLports" envisioned at the time by DHC and others, for the most part, failed to materialize, there were some noteworthy exceptions. For example, in Norway, a network of STOLports designed around the Twin Otter was built along that country's coastline, linking remote towns and villages with Oslo. The DHC-6 also brought airline service to Chicago's tiny lake front airport and to similar, short fields worldwide.

As the commuter airline industry grew, so too did the size of its airplanes. De Havilland developed the DHC-7 or "Dash 7," a 50-seat STOL transport, but as most commuter airlines no longer required STOL performance, the model enjoyed only limited success. Its successors, the 36-seat DHC-8 or "Dash 8" and 56-seat DHC-8-300, established good sales records and excellent reputations with the regional airlines that grew out of the commuters.

By 1988, the last of 844 Twin Otters had come off the production line. These airplanes have found homes with more than 300 operators in 90 countries, reflecting widespread recognition of the Twin Otter's unique set of capabilities. The outstanding reliability and favorable economics of the DHC-6 have contributed not only to the birth of the regional airline industry but also to Canada's growing reputation as a world leader in regional aircraft design and production.

Chapter 39
British Aerospace Jetstream 31 and 41

History is filled with examples of ideas that were ahead of their time. They are usually forgotten long before they have the opportunity to prove themselves, but in the case of the Jetstream 31 regional airliner, a great idea got a new lease on life a decade after a false start. Today the airliner has become one of the industry's best-selling airplanes and has even spawned a successful offspring.

The British Aerospace (BAe) Jetstream 31 started its career as the Handley Page H.P. 137 Jetstream. It was the last design to emerge from one of the world's most respected—and Britain's oldest—aircraft manufacturers. Frederick Handley Page was born in 1885, and after being educated as an engineer, formed his own airplane company in 1909. His first design, the two-seater Handley Page Type E, made its first flight in 1911. Though not a great commercial success, the model won praise from all who flew it.

The BAe Jetstream 31 is an improved design based on the Handley Page Jetstream. Note the external baggage pod slung under the airliner's belly. (British Aerospace)

The Jetstream 41 features a stretched fuselage, a new wing, more powerful engines, and many other improvements. (British Aerospace)

During the next 60 years, Sir Frederick (he was knighted in 1942) became known for some very remarkable aircraft, most of which bore his famous initials. In World War I, for example, the H.P. 0/400 created a sensation as one of the largest bombers of its time. After the war, a number of 0/400s were converted to civil airliners. But Handley Page, who had also founded his own airline, was not content on conversions — he was insistent on building a tailor-made commercial transport. The result was the 15-seat W8, which flew for his airline from London to both Brussels and Paris. This operation was later absorbed by Imperial Airways, a forerunner of today's British Airways.

By the 1930s, Imperial Airways was serving an extended system throughout Europe, the Middle East, and India — known as "Empire routes" — using the beloved Handley Page H.P. 42. Though slow and ungainly, the H.P. 42 became a legend in its own time, owing to its luxurious cabin and stellar reputation for safety. Eight of these four-engine airliners were eventually built.

Two more famous bombers, the Hampden and the Halifax, were produced by Handley Page during World War II. In the 1950s, the firm produced its last bomber, the elegant Victor, which was powered by four jet engines buried in a graceful, crescent-shaped wing.

The interior of a British Aerospace Jetstream 41. Note the three-abreast seating offered by the popular regional airliner. (British Aerospace)

But Handley Page continued to build transports too. The H.P. 68 Hermes was a four-engine piston-powered postwar airliner which enjoyed only limited commercial success, although over 150 were built for the Royal Air Force as Hastings. Likewise, the Handley Page Herald, a twin-engine turboprop similar in size and appearance to Fokker's F.27, failed to win many orders.

Sir Frederick died in 1962. He had participated in the company's decision-making all through its existence. But his dogged determination to keep Handley Page independent during the early sixties, when much of Britain's aircraft industry was going through "mergermania," would eventually be the firm's undoing. Oddly enough, the demise of Handley Page was directly linked to the Jetstream, which was an ironic twist, considering the airliner's later success.

The Jetstream was conceived in 1965 as a wide-body corporate aircraft and regional airliner. The idea behind the Jetstream was to provide corporate executives and commuter passengers with the same standard of comfort they had come to expect in larger airplanes. Unlike its competitors, the Jetstream featured a pressurized cabin with stand-up headroom, a small galley, and a lavatory—in addition to a cruising speed in excess of 300 mph. It also had a jet-like appearance with its swept tail and pointed nose. When the

Jetstream made its first flight on August 18, 1967, Handley Page held orders for 165 aircraft. The US Air Force later added eleven more to that total by ordering a military transport version.

Unfortunately, flight testing and development took longer than anticipated, delaying the company's revenue from the program. As a result, Handley Page experienced cash-flow problems, which it was unable to solve with its own resources. When Handley Page filed for bankruptcy in 1970, a proud name disappeared from the ranks of the world's great aircraft manufacturers.

But the Jetstream airliner did not disappear. Some three dozen aircraft had already been built, and in 1971 the newly established Jetstream Aircraft Limited took over production together with Scottish Aviation. The latter assumed complete control of the program a year later when the Royal Air Force ordered 26 Jetstreams for use as training aircraft. Meanwhile, the original Handley Page Jetstreams were making a name for themselves in the United States. They were a welcome relief for commuter passengers who had been accustomed to crawling through tiny Beech 99s and Fairchild Metros. But additional orders failed to materialize.

Then, on January 1, 1978, Scottish Aviation was absorbed by British Aerospace. The new parent organization took a careful look at the airplane and decided to relaunch the program that December as the Jetstream 31. This version featured new American-built Garrett powerplants, advanced avionics, and updated interiors. The Jetstream's second inaugural flight took place on March 18, 1982. Since then, over 400 aircraft have been sold, making the Jetstream 31 the world's best-selling, 19-seat, pressurized airliner.

At the 1989 Paris Air Show, BAe announced a new model—the Jetstream 41. This stretched version incorporated a number of important changes, including a new wing, more powerful engines, and ten more seats, for a total of 29. Its maiden flight took place on September 25, 1991, at which time British Aerospace held commitments for 115 aircraft. That number has increased to more than 150 Jetstream 41s, bringing the combined sales for both types to over 550. These sales totals reflect the Jetstream's balance of competitive performance, comfort, and reliability, as well as its low cost. Such are the marks of a successful airliner production program.

Despite the Jetstream's early stop-and-go career, time has vindicated the basic design. First flown 30 years ago, it should remain in service for many years to come. The model's success is a fitting tribute to the vision and legacy of one of aviation's greatest pioneers, Sir Frederick Handley Page.

Chapter 40
Boeing 747

In 1969, aerospace technology made several giant leaps. Although many remember it as the year Neil Armstrong became the first human to set foot on the moon, it was also the year that witnessed the first flights of the Concorde supersonic transport and the Boeing 747 "Jumbo Jet." From the air traveler's point of view, the 747 marked the beginning of the "Spacious Age." And of the three events, it could be argued that the maiden flight of the Boeing 747, on February 9, 1969, had both the most immediate and the longest-lasting impact on world culture. Economically transporting tens of thousands of passengers each day across continents and over oceans, the 747 has had the greatest influence in making the world a smaller place. Its stimulus to world trade and its immense size have sustained its role as the new "ocean liner" of the late 20th century.

Like those of Boeing's earlier planes, the Stratocruiser and 707, the 747's origins began with a military requirement. In 1964, the US Air Force identified a need for a

Large cargo doors and double-width passenger doors were designed to allow rapid loading and unloading of the huge Boeing 747. (Bill Mellberg)

The early 747s featured plush first class lounges on the upper deck. (Pan American Airlines)

giant cargo jet called the C–5A. Boeing, Douglas, and Lockheed each submitted proposals for the airplane. Although the contract to build the enormous military jet was granted to Lockheed the following September, Boeing's work was not in vain. The high-capacity Douglas DC–8 Super Sixty series and Boeing's own studies identified the growing need for a very large passenger jet. By October 1965, Boeing engineers were working on preliminary designs for the first of an entirely new breed of "wide-bodied" airliners, based on the company's design for the C–5A.

A variety of sizes, shapes, and design configurations was considered, with most calling for the 747 to be a double-decker. But because Boeing wanted to offer a variant as a pure freighter, a single-deck layout was eventually adopted with an upper deck at the forward end housing the cockpit and a small lounge. The lounge could be reached by a spiral staircase in a similar fashion to that on the Stratocruiser which Boeing had built two decades earlier. By placing the cockpit above the main deck, a hinged nose could be utilized on freighter versions, which would allow forward loading and unloading of bulky cargoes. Apart from these features, the four-engine 747 resembled a scaled-up 707. But its performance and dimensions would far surpass its famous predecessor.

Although able to use the same runways as 707s, the first 747s were half again as long and more than twice as heavy as the smaller jet. Each Pratt & Whitney JT9D engine on the 747 produced two and a half times as much thrust as the JT3D on the 707. The 747 featured 16 main landing gear wheels on four bogies compared to the 707's eight wheels and two bogies. There were twice as many lavatories and twice as many galleys to provide for more than double the number of passengers. Indeed, the biggest difference was the 747's nearly 20-foot wide cabin, which permitted the airplane to seat up to 490 passengers. As many as ten seats could be placed in each row, and two aisles ran through the cabin to permit easier access from each seat. The 747 was also 50 mph (ten percent) faster than the 707.

By the spring of 1966, Boeing's board of directors had made a tentative commitment to the 747 program. Although the potential economic rewards were enormous,

The Boeing 747's imposing size is apparent as the airliner emerges from a hangar. (Boeing)

the 747 represented an equally enormous financial risk for the company. Boeing's billion dollar investment required sales of 50 747s to reach the break-even point. However, the company's projections had envisioned a potential market for hundreds of 747s.

On April 13, 1966, Pan American World Airways placed the first order, for a fleet of 25 747s. Pan Am founder Juan Trippe was once again leading the way into a new era in aviation. Other carriers soon followed Pan Am's lead, and Boeing set about the gargantuan task of producing the world's largest jetliner. The first step was to build a giant new manufacturing plant at Paine Field in Everett, Washington, 30 miles north of Seattle. Likewise, across the continent at Middletown, Connecticut, Pratt & Whitney geared up to develop the world's most powerful jet engine, the JT9D, which would generate 43,500 pounds of thrust.

The first 747 took to the air on February 9, 1969, with Jack Waddell at the controls. His copilot was Brien Wygle, and Jess Wallick was the flight engineer. The high-bypass JT9D engines produced tremendous thrust but little noise and no smoke. The takeoff was more majestic than spectacular, reminiscent of a huge bird gracefully soaring into the clouds. The airplane received its FAA type certificate on December 30, 1969, and amidst much fanfare, entered service with Pan Am 23 days later between New York and London.

There were a number of early service problems with the 747, many attributable to its tremendous size. Most significantly, airport infrastructure had to catch up with aviation technology—disembarking more than 350 passengers simultaneously overwhelmed some airport terminals. But ground services soon adapted to the increase in passengers, while the 747's capacity relieved congestion in the air. Designed not so much to relieve congestion as to keep up with the growing demand for seats, Pan Am's 747s carried as many passengers across the Atlantic in their first six weeks of operation as the *Queen Mary* carried in eight months. Air travel was growing rapidly and would continue to grow as a result of lower fares made possible by the introduction of wide-bodied transports beginning with the 747.

Boeing updated and upgraded the 747 as it had its other jetliners. The heavier 747B (later called the 747-200) entered service in 1970, followed in 1973 by the short-range 747SR, designed primarily for high-density routes in Japan. Two freighter versions were offered, including one with a hinged nose. The long-range 747SP (Special Performance), shorter than earlier models by 48 feet, entered service in 1976. The 747-300, which made its debut in 1983, had an Extended Upper Deck (dubbed "EUD" by Boeing), which enabled airlines to seat 69 air travelers "upstairs" in place of a lounge, for a total of up to 624 passengers. The long-range 747-400 with extended tip winglets (and designed to be flown by only two pilots) entered service in 1989. Nearly three decades after its maiden flight, over 1,150 747s had been produced. The airplane should continue to be a bestseller. Boeing's jumbo gamble has generated jumbo results!

Chapter 41
McDonnell Douglas DC-10 and Lockheed L-1011

When Boeing announced its decision to produce the 747, some analysts believed the market for such a giant aircraft would be limited. They were wrong — the introduction of a wide-bodied transport on long-distance flights generated a demand for a similar jetliner on short- and medium-range air routes. American Airlines soon asked both Douglas and Lockheed to design a wide-bodied "air bus" for high-density markets such as its heavily traveled route between New York and Chicago. The airplane would need good short field performance for New York's La Guardia Airport but would also need to provide wide-body comfort for two to three hundred passengers. To improve economics, American also specified a twin-engine layout.

Talks with other carriers convinced both manufacturers that a trijet would have greater appeal, especially on over-water routes. Eastern Air Lines, for example, saw a role for such an airliner on its New York-San Juan route. As a result, Douglas and Lockheed

The tail-mounted position of the number two engine is readily apparent during the takeoff of this American Airlines DC-10. (American Airlines)

The fuselage-mounted number two engine and its "S-duct" air intake are apparent as the first Lockheed L-1011 TriStar lifts off the ground. (Lockheed)

produced designs that were larger than what American Airlines required though still considerably smaller than the 747. By the fall of 1967, Lockheed was ready to formally offer its new L-1011 TriStar to the airlines. Having delivered its last Electra in 1962, the company was eager to move forward with its first jetliner.

Meanwhile, despite a backlog of DC-8 and DC-9 orders, Douglas Aircraft had fallen on hard times. As 1966 drew to a close, a number of circumstances had put the proud firm on the brink of bankruptcy. The realization that only drastic measures could save the company resulted in its merger with McDonnell Aircraft of St. Louis, Missouri, in April 1967 to form the McDonnell Douglas Corporation. Although McDonnell was known primarily for building Phantom jet fighters and Gemini spacecraft, its founder, James McDonnell, had much in common with Donald Douglas. Both men were MIT graduates, and both had worked for Glenn L. Martin before setting off to found their own companies. McDonnell, known as "Mr. Mac," was determined to keep the corporation in the commercial aircraft business. Accordingly, he committed McDonnell Douglas to the DC-10, which, like the L-1011, was a wide-bodied trijet.

This pair of Northwest DC-10s, passing one another during takeoff and landing, are supported by the extra twin-wheel belly gear employed on the heavier overseas models. (Northwest Airlines)

The DC-10 and L-1011 emerged from the two corporate design offices as nearly identical twins. The only obvious difference was the location of the center engine. Lockheed mounted the engine on the TriStar at the rear of the fuselage in a manner not unlike the Boeing 727. Douglas engineers mounted the engine up on the tail, deleting the "S-duct" air intake, thus adding to the usable cabin space. The two airplanes also differed in their choice of engines—Douglas chose General Electric's new CF6, while Lockheed selected the somewhat more advanced Rolls-Royce RB.211. The TriStar featured several additional advanced systems which gave it a slight technological edge over the DC-10, although overall the two jetliners were similar in performance. But Douglas was prepared to compete more effectively on price.

The DC-10 drew first blood, winning an initial order from American Airlines for 25 DC-10s on February 19, 1968. The following month, Lockheed sold 50 TriStars to Eastern Air Lines, 44 to TWA, and 50 to Air Holdings, a British firm which would market them worldwide. One month later, United Air Lines bought 30 DC-10s. A great race was on! Douglas was first in the air with the maiden flight of the DC-10 at Long

Beach on August 29, 1970. The first L-1011 took off from Lockheed's giant new plant at Palmdale, near Edwards Air Force Base on November 16, 1970.

Early problems arose for the TriStar though not through any deficiencies in its own design. Cost overruns on the RB.211 jet engine drove Rolls-Royce into receivership; the TriStar's dependence on Rolls-Royce nearly did the same to Lockheed. Through most of 1971, while the L-1011 flight test program was proceeding smoothly, Rolls-Royce and Lockheed were both on roller coasters as the British and American governments negotiated rescue plans. A $250 million government loan guarantee, approved by a narrow margin that summer, saved the TriStar from extinction. But the uncertainty over the TriStar's future gave Douglas the opportunity to advance on its rival.

The DC-10 entered service with American Airlines between Los Angeles and Chicago on August 5, 1971. Eastern launched TriStar flights nearly nine months later on April 30, 1972. The DC-10 and L-1011 both proved to be very popular, but orders mounted slowly for both types. The DC-10 was offered from the outset in several different versions, including the long-range Series 30 and Series 40. Likewise, the TriStar was tailored to meet specific needs, the most significant variant being the long-range L-1011-500, which featured a longer wing and shorter fuselage. But the TriStar's early problems, together with a marked downturn in the world economy, contributed to disappointing sales. Production halted in 1984 after 250 TriStars had been built, including 50 L-1011-500s. Though it was an excellent airliner, the TriStar proved to be Lockheed's last effort at producing commercial aircraft.

The DC-10 also failed to generate the sales projected for it, partly because of the economic downturn and partly because of a series of unrelated but fatal crashes involving DC-10s. These well-publicized accidents tarnished the airliner's reputation and even grounded it for a time. Douglas delivered the last DC-10 in 1989 after 446 had been built, including 60 KC-10A tanker/transports for the US Air Force. Production shifted that same year to the McDonnell Douglas MD-11, a stretched and improved DC-10. By 1998, over 175 MD-11s had been sold. The last aircraft will come off the line early in the year 2000.

In the end, the DC-10 won its "Great Race" with Lockheed. But the contest had cost both firms dearly. Douglas and Lockheed learned the hard way that cooperation, not competition, is often the best course in an environment of limited resources and markets. This lesson had already been absorbed by their European counterparts, who were about to found the Airbus Industrie consortium, an event which would have a dramatic effect on the world jetliner business.

Chapter 42
VFW 614

When the Canadair Regional Jet took off on its maiden flight in 1991, it was described in the popular press as the first jet transport designed specifically for short-haul commuter routes. But another jet, tailored to the same market, had flown 20 years earlier. This airliner, the VFW 614, had been built in Germany, and it attracted attention largely for the unusual placement of its engines—above the wings! The VFW 614 failed to live up to its potential for a variety of reasons, and few people remember it today. But its story provides the important lesson that being first with a new technology is not always an advantage when it comes to selling airliners.

Vereinigte Flugtechnische Werke GmbH (VFW) was formed in 1963 as a consortium that included two more familiar names, Focke-Wulf and Weser Flugzeugbau. These were Bremen-based firms that through the end of World War II had produced a number of outstanding fighters, bombers, transports, and seaplanes. Ernst Heinkel Flugzeugbau,

The third VFW 614 prototype lands at Britain's Farnborough Air Show in 1974. (VFW-Fokker)

more fuel over shorter distances and at lower altitudes. But Britain and France were collaborating on a new jet engine called the M45H which promised to be more competitive. It was designed by Rolls-Royce and SNECMA to be quiet, rugged, reliable, economical, and easy to maintain. By 1968, the go-ahead had been given to complete the design work on both the airframe and the engine. The following year, three prototypes began taking shape at VFW's Bremen plant, and the first VFW 614 was rolled out on April 5, 1971.

VFW test pilot Leif Nielsen lifted the first 614 from the Bremen runway for its initial flight on July 14, 1971. The men and women who had designed and built the airplane watched with pride as their dream was finally realized. The maiden flight had followed years of delays, frustrations, and assorted economic, political, and technical problems. But after the triumphant first flight, the 614 program soon ran into trouble.

In October, the prototype experienced severe buffeting and vibration during a test flight, grounding the 614 for four months while engineers modified the tail section. On February 1, 1972, the airplane returned to the air for what was supposed to be a routine test. But toward the end of the flight, the 614 started shaking once again, and Nielsen told his crew to bail out. Both he and the flight engineer, Jurgen Hammer, landed safely. Unfortunately, copilot Hans Bardill was not so lucky. His parachute failed to open, and he fell to his death. The airplane crashed just a short distance away from the VFW plant at Bremen Airport.

This setback did not discourage VFW. The cause of the crash was traced to elevator "flutter," a problem which was quickly resolved. The other two prototypes resumed the test program, and the 614 soon proved to be a reliable airliner. VFW-Fokker's marketing department embarked on a series of demonstration tours, one of which resulted in the first 614 order from Cimber Air, a Danish regional carrier. Cimber bought two VFW 614s, received the first production aircraft in August 1975, and put it into service that November. At about the same time, VFW-Fokker announced additional orders from two French carriers, Air Alsace and TAT, for three and eight aircraft respectively. Things were looking up again!

However, apart from three airliners purchased by the German Luftwaffe, no further 614 orders were forthcoming. VFW explored several options, including a stretched 60-seat model. But in December 1977, the Board decided to halt production and terminate the program. The VFW 614s already in airline service were returned to the manufacturer, Fokker and VFW soon parted company, and VFW eventually became part of today's Daimler-Benz Aerospace.

Despite its protracted development, the VFW 614 was a capable aircraft. But most of the commuter airlines, for which it was developed, lacked both the finances and the traffic to support jet operations in 1977. As it turned out, the 614 had actually arrived about twenty years too soon!

Chapter 43
Airbus A300

American Airlines was not alone in looking for a twin-engine wide-bodied jetliner in 1966. European airlines had an even greater need for such an airplane on their short-haul high-density continental routes. British Aircraft Corporation and Hawker Siddeley Aviation had each studied concepts for such a design as had Sud-Aviation in France. The development costs for a large airplane were more than could be sustained by the resources of any single European manufacturer, and no European aircraft builder by itself had ever embarked on such an ambitious and risky project. Yet if Europe were to compete with America's Boeing, Douglas and Lockheed, it would need to produce large high-technology aircraft for the world market. Acting on these concerns, the British, French, and German governments in the fall of 1966 agreed to support the joint development of a twin-engine 250-seat "air bus" jetliner.

The sleek lines of the Airbus A300 are shown off in this view of a Continental Airlines airliner. (Continental Airlines)

A Kuwait Airways A300-600 in the skies over France during a pre-delivery flight from Toulouse. (Airbus Industrie)

The original partners, Sud-Aviation (later to be known as Aérospatiale), Deutsche Airbus GmbH (now a part of Daimler-Benz Aerospace), and Hawker Siddeley Aviation (now a part of British Aerospace) eventually adopted a design for a 300-seat airplane called the A300. It was to be powered by two all-new Rolls-Royce RB.207 engines. But the partners scaled back the design, renaming it the A300B, and chose General Electric CF6 powerplants instead, thus avoiding the engine problems that were to plague Lockheed's TriStar. The engine change cost the backing of the British government, but Hawker Siddeley remained in the program as a private venture. The Dutch firm, Fokker, and the Spanish firm, CASA, also joined the project as limited partners.

The A300B was officially announced at the 1969 Paris Air Show. A corporate entity, Airbus Industrie, was formed to manage the development, production, sales, and support of the airliner. Unlike the Concorde and other collaborative projects, there would only be a single final assembly plant at Toulouse in France. Fuselage sections would be built in Germany, wing-boxes in Britain, flaps and leading edges in Holland, engines in the US, and (later) doors and tail sections in Spain. All of these elements were to be brought together in France for final assembly by Super Guppy cargo planes—specially adapted Boeing 377 Stratocruisers. Each partner would have a share in the work, the risk, and the potential profits in proportion to their initial investment. The French and German governments would also be repaid for their prime role in financing the program. The Airbus consortium thus united the resources of Europe's leading aircraft manufacturers in a single international enterprise.

Despite the multinational nature of the A300 project, the development program proceeded quite smoothly, the first flight taking place on October 28, 1972. The A300 received its FAA type certificate on March 15, 1974. But while the technical problems were overcome and the plane was sound, Airbus Industrie was a newly-formed entity which lacked the credibility necessary for immediate success in the marketplace. Air France, a state-owned carrier, ordered six A300s in 1971 and inaugurated service between Paris and London on May 23, 1974. Germany's Lufthansa ordered three of the airliners in 1973; these entered service three years later. A handful of A300s were sold or

Airbus uses the outlandish-looking A300-600ST, a modified A300, for transport of large aircraft assemblies—such as complete wing sections—between members of the consortium. (Airbus Industrie)

leased to other European carriers as well as to a few airlines in Asia and Africa. But at the end of 1975, Airbus had only 33 firm orders. The drought continued for the next 16 months. Although the A300 filled a niche between the Boeing 727 and McDonnell Douglas DC-10, few airlines were willing to purchase it.

Experts were predicting Airbus' imminent collapse when Eastern Airlines' president and former Apollo astronaut, Frank Borman, announced his decision to lease four long-range A300B4s (the initial production models were A300B2s) on a trial basis. The lucrative North American market had finally been cracked. Borman liked the A300 and praised its performance, eventually placing 34 in Eastern's fleet. Although it took Airbus some time to further penetrate the North American market, the company earned much needed credibility with the Eastern purchase. By 1979, Airbus had firm orders or options for 256 airplanes from 32 customers. This remarkable turnaround marked the true beginning of one of aviation's greatest success stories.

To broaden its market, Airbus expanded its product line in 1978 by launching the 200-seat A310. The A310 had a shortened fuselage, a modified wing, and many other new and advanced systems. Its first flight took place from Toulouse on April 3, 1982. From the outset, Airbus had planned to produce a "family" of jetliners, thus emulating Boeing's successful strategy. The B10 variant of the A300 became the A310, and the B9 and B11 versions later took form as the A330 and A340. The basic A300B4 was likewise updated in 1980 as the "new and improved" A300-600.

The A300 fuselage with its twin-aisles and eight-abreast seating provided unmatched comfort on short- and medium-range routes. In 1987, its fuselage was lengthened and incorporated into the twin-engine A330 and four-engine A340 programs. A new wing makes these two airplanes, each of which can carry over 400 passengers, particularly suitable for long-range routes. The A340-300, the largest jetliner ever built in Europe and the only four-engine Airbus airliner, first flew in 1991, followed by the A330 a year later.

By 1997, 25 years after the A300's maiden flight, Airbus Industrie had sold some 750 A300s and A310s. More than 400 A330s and A340s had also been ordered. The airliner that no airline seemed to want had become a world-beating best-seller. And through the vision of its founders, the talent of its workers, and the quality of its products, Airbus Industrie has emerged as the world's second leading airliner manufacturer, eclipsing the former McDonnell Douglas and challenging Boeing for the lead.

The Airbus partners had correctly forecast the need for a family of economical twin-engine wide-bodied airliners. Once credibility had been established, sales soared, and the basic A300 proved to be one of the most "elastic" airplanes ever produced, with many variants on the original design. The success of Airbus Industrie is a monument to international cooperation, persistence, and technical skill.

Chapter 44
Airbus A320

Airbus Industrie established the foundation for a family of airliners like Boeing's with the wide-bodied A300. But without another line of smaller short- or medium-range jetliners, the Airbus family was not complete — or competitive. Both Douglas and Boeing had garnered huge orders for the Douglas DC-9 and Boeing 737 series. And in the early 1980s, they were still selling variants of those airliners for short- and medium-range routes. If Airbus was to make further progress in establishing itself as a major producer of jetliners, it would have to be able to offer something completely new. The A320 was the answer to this challenge.

In the decade following the establishment of Airbus, European aircraft manufacturers had studied a number of different proposals to produce a narrow-bodied 150-seat jetliner that could eventually replace Boeing 727s and 737s and DC-9s. A team composed of members from the Airbus partners, called the Joint European Transport group

Here is one of Air Canada's Airbus A320s during a pre-delivery flight over France. Note the wingtip fences for drag reduction—these are now standard on all Airbus airliners. (Airbus Industrie)

(JET for short), was formed in 1977 to define such an airliner. By 1980, their proposals were given the SA (Single Aisle) designation in Airbus literature. The SA2 was a 160-seat stretched version of the basic SA1 design.

Airbus Industrie did not intend to build a European imitation of the Boeing 737 or DC-9. The consortium wanted the SA2 to incorporate cutting-edge systems and technologies. Such a jetliner would represent a clear advance over the derivative designs coming out of Long Beach and Seattle, and could mount another bold challenge to American dominance.

Thus, the A320, as the SA2 project became known, would be the first commercial aircraft to abandon traditional control columns in favor of fighter-style sidestick controllers for the pilot and copilot. The cockpit would also feature six integrated CRT panel-displays instead of mechanical gauges and instruments. The A320 would be the first airliner to use computer flight controls, commonly referred to as "fly-by-wire." In these systems, electrical signals replace mechanical control of flying surfaces. Many other systems in the A320 would also be computerized, thus lowering fuel consumption and maintenance costs, easing operation and — most important for airlines — increasing profitability. Newly available materials would be used in the aircraft's structure, and an advanced-technology wing would add to overall performance. Finally, the A320's cabin with its six-abreast seating, would be wider than Boeing's narrow-bodies, setting a new standard for comfort.

In short, the A320 was designed from the ground up to be a state-of-the-art next generation jetliner. Initially, just one fuselage choice would be offered with seating for up to 160 passengers. Airlines could choose between the CFM56 engine developed jointly by General Electric and France's SNECMA, or the IAE V2500, produced by a consortium including Pratt & Whitney, Rolls-Royce, Germany's MTU, Italy's Fiat, and Japanese Aero Engines. Both powerplants produced 25,000 pounds of thrust.

At the 1981 Paris Air Show, Air France ordered 25 A320s and placed options on 25 more. A worldwide recession kept other carriers from placing additional orders, and Airbus decided to delay the decision to formally proceed with the program. The tide turned, however, when Prime Minister Margaret Thatcher agreed to loan British Aerospace the funds for its share of the investment in the A320, and the French and German governments followed suit. The official go-ahead was given in early 1984, and the order list soon began to grow. By the time the first A320 was rolled out in a spectacular ceremony on February 14, 1987 (with British Princess Diana there to christen it), the airplane had won more orders before a first flight than any other airliner in history. Sixteen customers had already bought 265 A320s with options on 174 more.

The gleaming silver and white A320 took off on its maiden flight eight days later, on February 22, 1987. Air France inaugurated A320 service on April 18, 1988. Just over a year later, Airbus Industrie delivered its 500th aircraft — an A320 — to Northwest Airlines. The newest Airbus had attracted orders from a number of other North American carriers, including Air Canada, America West, Braniff, Canadian Airlines, and Pan Am. Unfortunately, Pan Am's order was cancelled, although the airline did fly the A300 and A310 before financial problems resulted in its 1991 demise. United Airlines' decision in 1992 to lease up to 100 A320s was a triumph for Airbus—and a major blow to Boeing and American pride.

The inroads that Airbus was making on American airliner manufacturers became a campaign issue in the 1992 presidential elections. American politicians accused European governments of subsidizing Airbus Industrie to the extent that the consortium was able to price its airplanes below their true market value. This charge was first raised when Eastern Airlines ordered the A300 in the late 1970s. Airbus defended itself by pointing out that immensely profitable military contracts had in effect underwritten the American aircraft industry for many years. The Europeans also contended they were gaining ground for the simple reason that they were building high-quality airplanes. Indeed, this became apparent in 1994 when a Boeing official revealed that the US firm had tried to lease an A320 for static display at its Seattle area plant. The idea was to give Boeing employees a close-up look at the competition!

The Airbus A321, seen here in Alitalia colors, is a stretched A320 designed to compete with Boeing's 757. (Airbus Industrie)

The standard Airbus wingtip fence is just visible near the lower right of this view of this Swissair Airbus A319, a version of the A320 with a shortened fuselage. (Airbus Industrie)

The A321, a stretched version of the A320 seating up to 220 passengers, was launched in 1989. Its first flight was on March 11, 1993. Entering service in early 1994, its major competitor is the Boeing 757. Unlike the rest of the Airbus family, final assembly of the A321 takes place at Hamburg, Germany. Airbus is also building a shortened model, the Airbus A319 with seating for 124 passengers, to directly compete with the Boeing 737. The A319, A320 and A321 enjoy a high measure of commonality—for example, their common cockpits and fly-by-wire systems permit "cross crew qualifications" with the larger A330 and A340 wide-bodied jetliners.

Perhaps the best testimony to the A320 family's quality and competitiveness is an order book that had reached well over 1,700 aircraft by 1998. Although the airliner was plagued early on by several unfortunate accidents — resulting in some sensational and reckless stories in the popular press — investigations revealed that the A320 design was not at fault. Subsidy or no subsidy, Airbus Industrie has achieved its success through vision, hard work, and entrepreneurialism. And Europe has become an equal player in the world jetliner business.

Chapter 45
Boeing 757 and 767

By the mid-1970s, Boeing was the undisputed world leader in jetliner production, offering an entire family of transports ranging from the 707 to the 747. But the company knew that if it were to retain its leadership position, it could not afford to rest on its laurels. Thus Boeing's engineers and sales personnel were always assessing new aircraft designs and changing market conditions. At this point in time their strategy focused on two concepts: 1) a new wide-body twinjet dubbed the 7X7 which would fill a gap between the 727 and the DC-10/L-1011, and 2) a twin-engine derivative of the 727 called the 7N7 which would offer increased capacity, longer range, and lower costs. During the next few years, these proposals went through a number of changes. Banking its future on the new aircraft, Boeing wanted to be sure that the designs were right, and that they would meet the airlines' needs through the rest of the century—and beyond.

The wide-body 7X7 eventually became the 767, and the 7N7 emerged as the essentially all-new 757 narrow-body jet (it would have the same diameter fuselage as the 727/737). On July 14, 1978, United Airlines placed the first order for 30 767s with the first deliveries scheduled for 1982. The 767 had been awarded the sale after a close competition with Boeing's new rival, Airbus Industrie, which was offering a similar aircraft, the A310. The following month, British Airways and Eastern Airlines announced their decisions to buy 40 757s with deliveries beginning in 1983.

Thus Boeing now had two new projects in the works. The 767 would be built at the company's expanding Everett, Washington plant, where the 747 was being produced, and the 757 would replace the 727 on the production line at its Renton factory near Seattle about 60 miles away. To keep costs down and sales potential up, the firm strove to achieve a measure of commonality between the two types, especially in the cockpit area. The 757 and 767 flight decks would be nearly identical, thus allowing an airline's pilots to qualify simultaneously to fly both airliners. Features in the shared cockpit included on-board computer control systems and cathode ray tube (CRT) displays instead of the usual dials and flight instruments. The airplanes would also share similar wing shapes, designed to maximize efficiency and minimize fuel burn. Indeed, economy was a recurring theme when it came to the design of the two new jetliners. With fuel prices soaring, Boeing was determined to produce a new generation of transports that would be more sophisticated, yet more economical to operate than any existing jets.

Since the 767 program was launched first, it was several months ahead of the 757. The first 767 flight took place on September 26, 1981. Six airplanes were used in the 1,600 hour test program, culminating in the first delivery of a Pratt & Whitney-powered 767 to United Airlines on August 19, 1982. United put the type into service the following month on its Chicago-Denver route. Like other carriers, United emphasized the

The Boeing 757, the twinjet successor to Boeing's highly successful 727 trijet, has like its older sibling become a dependable airline workhorse. (America West Airlines)

new jet's fuel efficiency. As a seat pocket brochure put it, "United's 767 will be a true ally in the fight to hold down the cost of airfares."

The 767's cabin width was in between that of the narrow bodies (such as the Boeing 737) and the larger jumbo jets (such as the Boeing 747). It featured 2-2-2 seating in first class, and 2-3-2 seating in coach. As the United brochure explained, "On the twin-aisle 767, 88 percent of the seats are next to a window or an aisle. So there isn't much chance you'll be stuck in the middle."

While United chose the JT9D engine for its 767s, Delta chose General Electric's CF6. This model 767 was delivered in October 1982, with Delta service starting in December. All of the initial versions carried 216 passengers in a typical mixed-class configuration. Soon the 767 was flying with airlines around the globe.

Meanwhile, the 757's maiden flight had taken place on February 19, 1982. Five aircraft participated in the test program, and the first delivery was made to Eastern Airlines in late December, with scheduled service starting on January 1, 1983. British

Airways 757 flights followed a month later. Both carriers had chosen the Rolls-Royce RB211 to power their airliners, although the 757 was also designed to be equipped with the Pratt & Whitney PW2037. Delta started flying the Pratt & Whitney version in 1984.

While the 757's fuselage had the same cross-section as the older Boeing 707, 727, and 737, with six-abreast (3-3) seating, it provided a more comfortable cabin with ample space for carry-on luggage in newly-designed overhead bins. The jetliner can carry 186 passengers in a typical mixed-class configuration, or up to 218 in an all-tourist layout. With a 23-foot stretch, the 757-300, launched in 1996, can accommodate up to 289 passengers. Its first flight was on August 2, 1998.

The 757 and 767 were well-received by the traveling public, and Boeing's order book soon started growing, as did the number of model variants being offered. For example, the basic 767-200 was stretched by some 21 feet to create the 767-300, increasing maximum capacity to 290 passengers. Its first flight was on January 30, 1986. Extended range "ER" models of the 767 were also introduced, making twin-engine fuel efficiency a possibility on long-distance flights.

The Boeing 767 offers wide-body comfort and twin-engine economics. Here flies the standard length fuselage version, the 767-200. (Trans World Airlines)

An Aeromexico Boeing 757 strikes a pose which accentuates its long, narrow-body fuselage. (Aeromexico)

Boeing's sales of these models received a boost when limitations governing use of twin-engine airplanes over water were lifted. The established rule had called for twin engine airliners to remain within 60 minutes of an alternate landing field in case of an engine failure (which would leave them with but one functioning engine, which is enough to fly an airliner, but without a safety margin). As they proved their reliability, the time constraint was increased to 180 minutes for the 767-200ER and 767-300ER. Thus, the acronym "ETOPS" (Extended-range Twin-engine OPerationS) became familiar to world travelers, and the lucrative North Atlantic routes were opened to 767s. Soon, the 757 also received ETOPS approval for long-distance flights.

While Airbus Industrie has challenged Boeing's dominant position in the jetliner business, the 757 and 767 have helped the Seattle firm to retain its competitive edge. By 1998, over 900 757s had been sold, and 767 sales were well past the 750 mark. When added in with its 737, 747, and 777 orders, Boeing remains the undisputed world market champion.

Chapter 46
Saab 340 and 2000

The onset of the Jet Age—with a contribution from the growing interstate highway system—spelled the end of passenger railways as a major mode of cross-country travel in North America. By 1971, the US government had taken over most American passenger rail service under the Amtrak umbrella. Likewise, although the Canadian Pacific's "Canadian" had become something of a national symbol, the deficit-ridden transcontinental passenger rail service came under government control as part of VIA Rail Canada in 1978. The demise of railways meant that smaller North American cities and towns increasingly found themselves left out of national transportation networks. Regional airlines rose to this challenge during the late 1970s, providing links between these small communities and major airports (and world airways).

Most of the early regional (also known as "commuter") airliners were stretched versions of twin-engine executive aircraft. Among the most popular were the Beechcraft

This view of a Saab 340 in the livery of Trans World Express shows off the regional airliner's sleek lines. (Saab Aircraft)

The first Saab 2000 takes flight with its predecessor model, a Saab 340B in American Eagle colors.
(Saab Aircraft)

99, based on the Queen Air, and the Fairchild Metro—both 19-seaters. When de Havilland Canada introduced its 50-seat Dash 7 in 1978, many regional carriers felt the jump in size was a bit too much and a little too soon. There was an emerging need for an economical "in between" design seating 30 to 40 passengers. Around the world, a number of different manufacturers were preparing to meet that demand, including a Swedish company that most people associate with automobiles.

The name "Saab" actually stands for Svenska Aeroplan Aktiebolaget — "Swedish Airplane Company." "Aktiebolaget" is usually shortened to "AB," explaining the abbreviated name by which the firm is commonly known. Founded in 1937 to produce airplanes for the Royal Swedish Air Force, Saab has earned its reputation as one of the world's most innovative airplane builders. In 1948, it produced Europe's first swept-wing jet fighter, the Saab 29 Tunnan. Then the Saab 35 Draken pioneered the double-delta wing that Lockheed eventually adopted for its triplesonic SR–71 Blackbird. The first use of canard wings in fighter jet design came with the Saab 37 Viggen. Saab's newest fighter, the Gripen, maintains Sweden's place at the leading edge of aviation technology with its advanced structures and computerized systems.

Saab's initial entry into the commercial aircraft business came in 1944 with the Saab 90 Scandia, a short-haul airliner that resembled a scaled-down Convair 240. Work halted on the Scandia and other commercial projects as the Cold War heated up, and the Swedish government pressed Saab to concentrate on military projects. Scandia production was transferred to Holland's Fokker in 1951. By that time, the project was effectively doomed. Only 18 Scandias were built, despite its sound design.

Saab continued to study commercial designs while concentrating on military aviation. In the early 1970s, Saab's market research identified a large demand for a turboprop regional airliner. Since the company had no recent experience selling civil transports, a search was begun for a risk-sharing partner to help produce the airliner. In 1979, negotiations were initiated with Maryland-based Fairchild Industries. Fairchild was a logical choice, given its participation with Fokker on the F-27 as well as the success of its own Metro commuter airliners.

The Saab 340 featured a stand-up cabin with overhead luggage bins, a full-size lavatory, as well as provisions for hot meal galley service. (Saab Aircraft)

In January 1980, Saab and Fairchild signed an agreement to "jointly develop, produce and market a new regional airliner." Saab had decided that the design should be modern, yet relatively simple. Low operating costs and high passenger acceptance were key factors. The airplane would be able to accommodate 35 passengers. General Electric's CT7 turboprop powerplant was chosen because of its low fuel consumption and low weight. The first customer contract was signed in November 1980, and Saab soon started building a new 269,000 square foot factory at Linköping for production of the Saab Fairchild SF340. It was completed in under 18 months.

As the SF340 design was refined, the two partners chose advanced, all-digital avionics for the cockpit and included a pressurized "stand-up" cabin with three-abreast seating. A full-size lavatory, overhead luggage bins, and a hot galley were intended to provide "wide-body comfort" on regional airline routes. Fairchild would manufacture the wings and tail sections while Saab was responsible for building the fuselages and for final assembly of the airplanes.

The first SF340 was rolled out in the presence of King Carl XVI Gustaf in October 1982. The maiden flight took place on January 25, 1983. Crossair of Switzerland inaugurated service on June 14, 1984. The first passenger was Pope John Paul II, who flew around Switzerland in a Crossair 340 during an official papal visit.

Because of financial problems, Fairchild withdrew from the project in 1985. Saab-Scania (Saab had merged with the Swedish bus and truck manufacturer Scania in 1968) took sole responsibility for production and by the fall of 1987 was turning out the first all-Swedish Saab 340s. In 1988, the firm decided to expand the product line by launching a stretched 50-seat variant called the Saab 2000.

By 1997, Saab had sold over 500 airplanes, including 454 Saab 340s and 60 Saab 2000s. The first 2000 took to the air on March 26, 1992. With a cruising speed in excess of 400 mph, it was designed to compete with the new regional jetliners that were being built by Canadair and Embraer. Unfortunately, the projected sales of the 2000 never materialized; and as 340 sales tapered off, Saab made the decision, in early 1998, to shut down both production lines by mid-1999. But given the popularity of the airplanes with passengers and crews—as well as airline accountants—the Saab "turbos" should remain in service for many years to come.

Chapter 47
de Havilland Canada Dash 7 and Dash 8

The name given to de Havilland Canada's popular Dash 8 twin-engine turboprop regional transport implies speed and efficiency, qualities which make the airliner ideal for busy executives who need to "dash" between cities for important meetings. But the name was not the clever concoction of a Madison Avenue advertising agency. It is simply the aircraft's corporate product number, the DHC-8 being de Havilland Canada's eighth indigenous design. Although the company's first six products had been named for Canadian mammals (the Chipmunk, Beaver, Otter, Caribou, Buffalo, and Twin Otter), that custom had been abandoned with the DHC-7 Dash 7 in 1973.

While de Havilland's earlier aircraft had been designed primarily for back country flying, the Dash 7 was envisaged as a modern 50-seat regional transport. It did, however, retain one important feature of its predecessors, the capacity for short takeoff and landing (STOL) operations. Having established itself as the world's leading manufacturer of

Air Wisconsin was an early Twin Otter customer and one of the first to operate the 50-seat Dash 7. (Bombardier Regional Aircraft)

A standard 36-seat Dash 8 Series 100 awaits ground service. This particular model is flown by Seattle-based Horizon Air. (Terry Shwetz/de Havilland Canada)

STOL airplanes, de Havilland Canada designed the capability into the new Dash 7, thus enabling the type to utilize small city center airstrips. The concept was put to the test starting in 1974 with a demonstration service called "Airtransit" between Montreal and Ottawa. Six DHC-6 Twin Otters were modified to approximate the comfort levels anticipated in the forthcoming Dash 7. A parking lot near downtown Montreal, and the historic Rockcliffe airport just east of Ottawa's city center, were converted to "STOLports" for the successful two-year experiment. With a bus ride at either end, the downtown-to-downtown travel time between the two cities was reduced to just over an hour, a considerable improvement over other alternatives. The success of the demonstration meant that de Havilland could now offer an entirely new concept in air travel. Time-conscious passengers could look forward to avoiding congested large airports in favor of city center STOLports in markets such as Chicago and Toronto. At the same time, the Dash 7 would offer the conveniences people had come to expect from modern airliners, namely a pressurized cabin, plenty of leg and headroom, beverage service, carry-on luggage bins, and a lavatory compartment. In addition, its four Pratt & Whitney Canada PT6A-50 engines were exceptionally quiet, making the airplane acceptable in highly-populated areas.

The Dash 7's maiden flight took place on March 27, 1975. It could take off and land from 2,000 foot runways, which is remarkable for a 50-seat airliner. The type went into service on February 3, 1978. Unfortunately, few carriers had a need for STOL transports, and few cities were willing or able to build new STOLports. Despite some notable exceptions, such as London's City Airport, where a runway was built on a former dock just minutes away from the banking district and the West End, DHC was unable to develop a larger market for the Dash 7. Production ended in 1988 after 114 Dash 7s had been built.

By 1980, it had become clear that the former commuter airlines were quickly becoming regional air carriers, connecting small and medium-size communities to hub airports in major cities. They needed an airliner in between the smaller Twin Otter and Dash 7 in size. They were also willing to sacrifice STOL performance for speed. Thus, de Havilland launched an new airliner incorporating these demands, the rakish Dash 8. The DHC-8 was powered by two Pratt & Whitney Canada PW120 turboprop engines. Like its predecessor, the new airplane was designed with short-haul comfort in mind. It provided a pressurized cabin for 36 passengers, and featured contoured seats and plenty of headroom. The first Dash 8 took off from de Havilland's Downsview plant on June 20, 1983.

By the time the trim, high-wing airliner entered service in December 1984, it had plenty of competition. The 35-passenger Saab 340 had flown in June, while Embraer's 30-seat EMB-120 "Brasilia" had made its maiden flight in July. Avions de Transport Regional (better known as ATR) flew their 50-seat ATR 42 the following year. In this crowded field, de Havilland had at least one genuine advantage; whereas its rivals were relative newcomers to the regional airline market, de Havilland had an established reputation for quality and dependability, earned during the Twin Otter's heyday with commuter carriers. In addition, the Canadian firm also had a well-established customer base.

In the mid- and late 1980s, the competition continued to heat up. In an attempt to capture a bigger share of the growing market, ATR launched the ATR 72, a 74-seat stretched version of the ATR 42, in 1985. In 1986 De Havilland responded with its own Dash 8 Series 300, another stretched model. The new 56-seat variant first took to the air on May 15, 1987, and airline deliveries began in February 1989. Meanwhile, Saab announced another stretched aircraft, the 50-seat Saab 2000, in 1988. And DHC started work on the Dash 8Q-400, a 70-seater, in 1995. It made its first flight on January 31, 1998, and is scheduled to enter airline service in 1999.

The competition in the regional transport market has been intense from the beginning, and the battle for market shares is still being waged. By 1998, de Havilland had sold over 550 Dash 8s to some 70 operators around the globe, including a number of military and executive models. ATR and Saab could claim roughly the same sales total in their

The 56-seat Series 300 was the first stretched version of the Dash 8, entering service in 1989.
(Charles Bryant/de Havilland Canada)

order books, while Embraer held a somewhat smaller share of the market. But they had all correctly identified the need for a high-speed turboprop regional airliner.

For DHC, the decision to abandon the Dash 7 in favor of the Dash 8 proved to be a good one. Today, de Havilland Canada is part of the Montreal-based Bombardier corporation, which also owns Canadair. Thus, Bombardier's Regional Aircraft Division produces both the turboprop Dash 8 and the jet-powered Canadair Regional Jet, offering regional carriers a choice of airplanes to meet their specific needs. The Dash 8 remains in production at Downsview, and the type has maintained and added to its enviable record for reliability. Pilots appreciate its high-speed performance, accountants like its low operating costs, and passengers enjoy its comfortable cabin. All in all, the DHC-8 is a real winner. And, like its famous predecessors, it ought to be giving dependable service for a long time to come.

Chapter 48
Canadair Regional Jet

The last step in the evolution of the Jet Age proved to be the most difficult. While many of today's passengers wince when they see an airliner with propellers, economics has always favored propjets on short-haul commuter flights. This simple and apparently inexorable fact made producing a small, pure jet transport for these routes a seemingly impossible dream. That is, until 1992, when a sleek, Canadian-built transport became the first jetliner to bring affordable jet travel to even the shortest of commuter runs. With this accomplishment, the Canadair Regional Jet has already left its mark on aviation history.

Canadair was founded in 1923 as the aircraft division of Canadian Vickers, the North American branch of Britain's giant Vickers defense organization (builders of ships, guns, and airplanes). During World War II, the Canadian firm produced more than 350 Consolidated PBY amphibians under license for Commonwealth forces. In 1952, the com-

Ohio-based Comair, a Delta Connection regional airline, has the largest "RJ" fleet, having ordered 150 of the sleek jets. (Bombardier Regional Aircraft)

pany became a part of the General Dynamics Corporation, and built hundreds of air-planes, from small jet trainers to large turboprop transports. Canadair was purchased by the Canadian government in 1976, and was sold to Bombardier ten years later. Bombardier was a Montreal-based firm known for its snowmobiles, railroad equipment, and a host of other hi-tech industrial and consumer products. In addition to Canadair, Bombardier also owns de Havilland at Downsview, Learjet in Wichita, and Short Brothers in Belfast, Northern Ireland. These subsidiaries give the company a very broad base in aerospace manufacturing experience and expertise.

The origins of the "RJ" reach back to William P. Lear, one of America's most inventive entrepreneurs. It was Bill Lear who developed the car radio (he founded Motorola), produced the first stereo tape players for automobiles, and came up with the idea for a small, high-speed business jet. When the first "'Lear Jet" took off in 1963, it started a revolution in corporate air travel. To date, more than 1,500 Learjets have been produced.

One of Lear's last projects (he died in 1978) included a new class of wide-body business jets which could seat up to 19 passengers in a true "stand up and walk around"

The Canadair Regional Jet, or "RJ," is based upon the same airframe as that of the Canadair Challenger, shown here. (Canadair)

Air Canada bought two dozen Canadair Regional Jets to develop its new trans-border routes between Canada and the United States. (Air Canada)

cabin. Whereas the original Lear Jet had set a new standard for speed, the "'LearStar 600" would set a new standard for comfort. Lear sold his concept to Canadair in Montreal in 1976, and the Canadian company refined, developed, and marketed the design as the CL-600 "Challenger."

The Canadair Challenger first flew on November 8, 1978, just two years after the program was launched. Since then, five basic versions have been produced, and the airplane has proven to be reliable, fuel efficient, quiet, and extremely popular with corporate executives. Some 350 Challengers have been sold to operators worldwide.

Both Bill Lear and Canadair saw another role for his LearStar 600. From the beginning, it was clear that the airplane's cabin was wide enough to accommodate four seats per row. By stretching the fuselage and adding some rows, up to 50 passengers could be carried in a commuter version. However, Canadair wisely focused initially on establishing the Challenger, thus gaining experience not only in building the jet, but also in supporting it. And both the airplane and the manufacturer developed a reputation for dependability. But Canadair engineers continued to study an airliner model of the Challenger, and the company's sales personnel continued to test the marketplace. Finally, in March 1989, the Regional Jet program was officially announced. The maiden flight took place from Dorval in Quebec on May 10, 1991.

The RJ makes use of the basic Challenger airframe, while adding some 20 feet to its length and five feet to its wing span. The same quiet, fuel-efficient General Electric CF-34 turbofan engines were utilized, along with a number of other common systems and components. Greater fuel capacity and enhanced avionics were added for airline operations. But despite these changes, the family resemblance between the two types remains apparent even at first glance. Although the RJ's cabin is not quite as luxurious as the Challenger's, it is every bit as comfortable as its competitors in the regional jet market. However, when it comes to performance, the RJ has no real competition. It is speedier than both the ATR 42 and the Saab 2000, by 200 and 100 mph, respectively, and can easily outrun Embraer's rival EMB-145. The Regional Jet is also vibration-free and provides a smooth quiet ride at altitudes up to 41,000 feet.

The first RJ was delivered to Lufthansa CityLine on October 19, 1992, and entered service 13 days later. Others soon followed, and by 1998 over 500 Regional Jets had been sold to some two dozen carriers.

While the RJ has found a home with regional airlines such as Sky West and Comair (the biggest operator with 70 jets in service), it has also carved a niche with major carriers such as Air Canada. Beginning in October 1994, Air Canada added 24 RJs to its fleet, using the 50-seat airliner to develop new trans-border routes between city pairs such as Ottawa and Chicago, and Toronto and St. Louis. Because traffic volume in these markets could not support a larger jet, such as a DC-9, flying the RJ gave the Canadian airline a distinct edge over its competitors.

The RJ has also given regional airlines new growth opportunities. Shortly after placing the Regional Jet into service, one airline chief executive said, "I have to tell you that we underestimated the passenger appeal of this airplane. I think it is going to completely change our method of doing business and the way customers perceive our operations." In many cases, the Regional Jet can offer point-to-point service on selected routes or increase the operational radius from hub airports, thus allowing regionals to develop new markets while improving service on others.

The Canadair Regional Jet has succeeded where others have failed by virtue of its advanced technology, low operating costs, high productivity, jet performance, and tremendous passenger appeal. Its timing was right as well, since a number of regional airlines were finally ready to enter the Jet Age when it came to market. As the RJ continues to prove itself, Canadair's order list is growing longer, and the long-term sales prospects for the streamlined "minijet" are looking better than ever.

Chapter 49
Boeing 777

At the dawn of the Jet Age, speed was one of the most important factors driving airliner development. But 40 years after the de Havilland Comet introduced jet travel to the world, economics had supplanted speed as the primary concern among airline executives responsible for purchasing airliners. Thus in 1969, the first "jumbo jet," the Boeing 747, started another revolution in mass transportation by making air travel more affordable. The demand for seats continues to grow with each passing year, which is what prompted Boeing to formally announce the newest member of its jetliner family—the 777—on October 29, 1990.

The 777 is the world's largest twin-engine transport, and is second only to the 747 in overall dimensions. Designed to replace DC-10 and L-1011 trijets as well as early model 747s, the 777 offers twin-engine economy with greater capacity than other twinjets on long-range flights. It also helps to maintain Boeing's competitive position with respect to Airbus Industrie's A330 and A340. Partly reflecting the fact that jetliner manu-

The Boeing 777 is the world's largest twin-engine transport. The unusual six-wheel main landing gear "bogies"—which attach the wheels to the struts—are barely visible here. (Airliners America)

The standard 777-200 can seat up to 440 people in an all-economy layout. The stretched 777-300 will accommodate as many as 550 passengers. (Boeing)

facturers are responding to similar market pressures, the A330 and 777 appear very similar to the casual observer.

The 777 was initially conceived as a 767 derivative called the 767-X. But after Boeing decided to seek more input from some of its potential customers, eight of the world's major airlines helped the company to redefine the 777, and "Working Together" became the project's official slogan. As a result, stretched versions of the 767 were rejected in favor of an all-new airplane, providing the widest cabin of any twinjet.

In a number of respects, the design and production of the 777 was highly innovative. For example, it was the first airliner to be completely designed using computers. Whereas in the "old days" engineers sprawled over drawing boards and produced wooden mockups of new airplanes, Boeing used more than 2,200 work stations and eight IBM mainframe computers to design and manufacture the 777. In addition, lightweight composite materials make up a significant percentage of the jetliner's structure, which along with the shape of its highly-efficient wing, maximizes fuel economy for the huge jetliner. Other new features include six wheels on each of the main landing gears, flat panel liquid crystal displays (LCDs) rather than cathode ray tube (CRT) screens in the cockpit, computerized '"fly-by-wire" flight controls, and optional folding wingtips which enable the 777 to take up less gate space at overcrowded airports (however, as of 1998, no carrier had specified this very unique option).

In the cabin, the airplane's layout offers passengers roomier seats, taller ceilings, more shoulder room, and gives airlines greater flexibility in locating galleys, toilets, and closets. Like other wide-body jets, the 777 has twin aisles. First class has luxurious 2-2-2 seating, business class offers 2-3-2 or 2-4-2 seating, and economy class can be set up in a variety of configurations with as many as ten seats per row. Typically, the 777 accommodates 305 passengers in three classes, or up to 440 in an all-economy version. A wide range of personal service options are available, such as telephones (which enable passen-

United Airlines placed the first order for the Boeing 777. Pictured here is the delivery ceremony for their service-inaugurating 777 airliner. (Boeing)

gers to make calls, send faxes, and relay computer data worldwide), individual TV screens with six video channels, and 19 CD-quality audio channels.

To power the twinjet, Pratt & Whitney, General Electric, and Rolls-Royce each offered what were the most powerful aircraft engines ever produced. The PW4000, GE90, and Trent 800 series each generate an average of 75,000 pounds of thrust, with growth versions going as high as 90,000 pounds. By comparison, the JT9D, which powered the original 747, produced 43,500 pounds of thrust. The new engines are also quite large; the GE90, for example, is nearly as wide as a 737 fuselage. Yet, despite their enormous size and awesome power, these hi-tech powerplants are exceptionally quiet.

Boeing identified two different markets for the basic 777-200—the "A-Market," which takes in high-capacity domestic flights, and the "B-Market," which focuses on long- distance overwater trips. The company also envisions a "C-Market" geared to ultra long-range global routes.

United Airlines placed the first order for 34 777s on October 15, 1990, followed by the official program launch two weeks later. As Boeing prepared for production of its latest jumbo jet, the company took on some new risk-sharing Japanese partners. On May 21, 1991, Fuji, Kawasaki, and Mitsubishi signed an agreement making them responsible for producing 20 percent of the airframe. In addition to sharing the risks, the arrangement also promises 20 percent of the rewards.

The first 777 was unveiled at a day-long celebration for Boeing customers and employees on April 9, 1994. The words "Working Together" were painted on its nose. Chief pilot John Cashman took the airplane on its successful maiden flight from Boeing's Everett plant on June 12, 1994. He reported that the 777 flew "as smooth as can be." Nine airplanes eventually participated in the extensive flight test program which included all three engine types.

United Airlines received its first airplane during a formal ceremony at Seattle's Boeing Field on May 17, 1995. The 777 entered scheduled service a few weeks later, and deliveries to other airlines soon followed. By the end of that year, Boeing's order book included some 250 777s. This list continues to grow, as does the jetliner itself. The stretched 777-300, which entered service in 1998, is the world's longest airliner at just over 242 feet. With up to 550 seats, it will carry as many passengers as the early 747s, while burning one-third less fuel.

Boeing is also considering a shortened version of the 777 with even longer range. Its continuing competition with Airbus obligates the company to consider every possible niche, which is why flexibility was built into the 777 design from the outset. Although the 777 appeared after other wide-bodied jetliners, such as the McDonnell Douglas MD-11 and Airbus A330 and A340, Boeing—and many others—believe the 777 is the "preferred airliner" in its class. As such, it has set a new standard that will carry the air transport industry into the 21st century.

Chapter 50
British Aerospace/Aérospatiale Concorde

When the Cunard Line's *Queen Elizabeth 2* set sail on her maiden voyage across the North Atlantic on May 2, 1969, she was the last in a long line of magnificent ocean liners. The QE2 carried 1,400 passengers from Southampton, England, to New York on that trip, which took 4 days, 16 hours and 35 minutes. Although the French Line's elegant S.S. France — the world's longest ocean liner — was still plying the Atlantic at the time, by 1974 the QE2 was the only passenger ship sailing between the Old and New Worlds. She offered passengers who had the time a nostalgic look at the past.

Two months to the day before the *QE2's* maiden voyage, an incredible, new "ocean liner"—just as graceful—took off on her maiden flight from Toulouse, France. A joint effort of Britain and France, the fabulous Concorde was the world's first supersonic transport. While the *QE2* needed four days to cross the North Atlantic, the Concorde was designed to make the 3,600-mile trip at 58,000 feet in just over three and a half

To celebrate the Concorde's tenth anniversary in service with British Airways, the airline commissioned a series of special photographs, including this one of four Concordes flying in formation. (British Airways)

The Concorde's needle-shaped fuselage and gently curved delta wing make the "Queen of the Skies" a work of art as well as a technological wonder. (British Airways)

hours. This compares to the 33½ hours Charles Lindbergh needed to fly the route in 1927. It had taken nearly seven years for the Concorde to get into the air for the first time, and it would take another seven long years of testing before the Concorde finally entered routine daily service.

Time is really what the Concorde is all about. Indeed, the graceful supersonic transport has been referred to more than once as a time machine. The premium fares paid to fly the Concorde are worth it to people in a hurry who can afford the expense of this most sophisticated and complex jet transport. From the Wright Brothers to the Space Shuttle, engineers have been developing flying machines that travel faster and faster. Most of the steps have been incremental ones, involving modest increases in speed with each new design. But with the development of jet engines during World War II, sleek new airplanes suddenly achieved speeds greatly exceeding their propeller-driven predecessors. The British had taken the lead in applying this new technology to civil air transport with the Comet. The French Caravelle likewise took early advantage of jet propulsion. By the early 1960s, designers in both countries were laying plans for the next logical step—a supersonic airliner.

For a long time, many engineers had thought that breaking the sound barrier was impossible because the build up of air in front of an airplane as it approached the speed of sound would tear it apart. A number of pilots lost their lives when their airplanes disintegrated as they approached the speed of sound. Tests showed that the compression of air in front of the airplane, while having little effect on the nose and fuselage of high-speed airplanes, wreaked havoc on their wings. This explained why rockets and bullets had no problem in breaking the sound barrier. But on October 14, 1947, US Air Force Captain Charles "Chuck" Yeager finally broke the sound barrier in the specially-de-signed, rocket-powered Bell X-1. The speed of sound was soon doubled and tripled by experimental rocket planes such as the X-1 and X-2.

Although the lessons learned from these flights were soon applied to the newest jet fighters, the design of a supersonic airliner presented special challenges. Unlike military jets, a supersonic transport would have to provide a shirtsleeve environment for its passengers and crew. It would need long-range capabilities, and it would also have to address the difficult problem of sonic booms, the annoying thunderclaps heard by those on the

Six of British Airways' seven Concordes are gathered together in this dramatic overhead view, which proves that the airliner is a object of beauty from every angle. (British Airways)

ground as a supersonic airliner passes overhead. Atmospheric friction—and the resultant overheating of the airliner's skin—were other problems facing engineers.

British and French engineers, working independently on the design of a supersonic airliner, had devised similar solutions to these problems. The staggering development costs of a supersonic transport—and of the engines to power it—led the two countries to sign an agreement in 1962 calling for the joint design, development, and manufacture of such an aircraft. British Aircraft Corporation and France's Sud-Aviation (later Aérospatiale) were assigned the task while Bristol-Siddeley (later Rolls-Royce) and France's SNECMA were chosen to produce the powerful new Olympus jet engines. The partners managed to overcome the language barrier, two different systems of measurement, and assorted political problems. But one problem remained. During the roll-out ceremonies at Toulouse in 1967, the British Minister of Technology, Anthony Wedgewood Benn, joked, "Only one disagreement has occurred during the years of cooperation with France. We were never able to agree on the right way to spell "Concord"—with or without an 'e.' I have decided to solve the problem myself. The British Concorde shall from now on also be written with an "e," for this letter is full of significance… Excellence, England, Europe, and Entente." He might have added, "Expensive!"

The first flight of the French-built Concorde was on March 2, 1969, followed by that of the first British-built Concorde one month later. Three years after that, Air France and British Airways became the only airlines to buy Concordes. Political interests and environmental concerns led to the demise of Boeing's planned supersonic transport and also resulted in the banning of the Concorde from most routes. As a result, only 20 Concordes were built—ten at BAC's huge Filton plant and ten at Toulouse. Only 14 entered service, with seven going to each carrier. Inaugural flights occurred simultaneously on January 21, 1976. Supersonic flight for paying passengers had become a reality!

The speed of sound varies with both temperature and altitude, which can lead to confusion. At sea level on a mild day, it is roughly 760 mph. At 35,000 feet, the altitude at which supersonic planes are designed to fly, it is approximately 660 mph. The speed of sound has been termed "Mach 1" in honor of Ernst Mach, the Austrian scientist who explained much of the physics of sound. Mach 2, at the altitudes and conditions practical for supersonic flight, is equivalent to 1360 mph—roughly the Concorde's cruising speed.

The Concordes have served well. Millions of Concorde passengers have enjoyed the truly unique experience of traveling faster than a speeding bullet while dining on fresh fruit, lobster, and fine wine. Only the bulkhead mounted Machmeter reading "M 2.00" and the Earth's curvature outside the window remind one how fast and how high the airplane flies. Like the *QE2*, the Concorde is not for everyone. But for over a quarter of a century, this magnificent "Queen of the Skies" has reigned supreme and has given all of us a preview of future airliner designs.

Afterword

Of the hundreds of different airliners that have been built and flown over the years, I have attempted to single out those which made the greatest contributions to the development of the commercial aviation industry. I have also included some aircraft, such as the DC-4E and Avro Canada C102 Jetliner, which, despite carrying few or no paying passengers, marked important milestones in aviation history and technology. All of the airliners selected for *Famous Airliners* have played a role in the evolution of today's remarkable globe-girdling air transport system.

Having looked at the past and present, I shall now attempt to conjure the future while remaining mindful that many previous projections about the course of aviation have been wanting. In 1942, for example, aviation writers looking ten years ahead fore-saw giant flying boats and helium-filled dirigibles. These soothsayers failed to recognize that the development of jet propulsion during the war years would lead to the introduc-tion of the de Havilland Comet in 1952. And a quarter of a century ago, many experts believed the supersonic transport (or SST) would be today's dominant type of long-range airliner, speeding passengers across the world's oceans in half the time of ordinary jets. Indeed, the Concorde has demonstrated the technical feasibility of supersonic travel. But the economic feasibility of supersonic flight has yet to be proven. The Concorde simply consumes too much fuel while carrying too few people to make it a truly prac-tical proposition. And while the airliner earns prestige for its operators, the lack of any additional orders tells the real story; without government support, the graceful Concorde would never have entered service.

Supersonic air travel may yet be around the corner. Expanding trade on the Pacific Rim would greatly benefit from faster travel, and a second generation SST linking the Americas with Asia and Australia could reduce the long flight times on current air routes. Likewise, the Concorde could be replaced by a more efficient SST over the Atlantic. New technologies may produce an aircraft with better economics and superior performance, although the environmental effects of high-flying jetliners on the upper atmosphere still pose a challenge for engineers. The development costs for a new super-sonic transport are staggering, and given the limited market, it is likely to be a coopera-tive international project. The United States, Europe, Russia, and Japan—all of whom are studying various concepts for such an airliner—might participate jointly in an SST project. Given a commitment by the turn of the century, a new SST could be flying by 2005.

Of course, the noise from sonic booms might still preclude supersonic flights over land. But aircraft designer Jim Floyd—who wrote the Foreword to this book—proposed a "no boom" SST in the early 1960s. At the time, he was chief engineer of Hawker Siddeley Aviation's Advanced Projects Group in England. His team came up with a

Mach 1.15 SST called the Type 1011 (not be confused with the Lockheed L-1011). The size and shape of the 160-seat swing-wing jetliner was such that the shock wave it generated would never have reached the ground. The Type 1011 could have flown across continents as well as over oceans, and while it would have been slower than the Concorde, it would have been 25 to 30 percent faster than subsonic commercial jetliners, thus cutting travel times considerably on long-distance routes. Moreover, Floyd's design made use of existing technology and could have been put into service quickly and economically. But the focus in the 1960s was on a Mach 2.0 SST, and the Type 1011 never got past the design study stage. Perhaps someone will dust off the idea and return it to the light of day sometime soon.

Meanwhile, the real trend in commercial aviation during the past quarter century has been toward greater economy rather than faster flight. And because developing a new airliner from scratch is so enormously costly, existing designs have been repeatedly stretched and otherwise modified in order to provide enhanced or specialized performance at a reasonable price. Thus, the original twin-engine medium-range A300 "air bus" has grown into the four-engine long-range A340. Similarly, the original 80-seat Douglas DC-9 short-haul jet has progressively evolved into the 172-seat McDonnell Douglas MD-90. Adding more fare-paying passengers by stretching the fuselage and installing uprated engines can reduce the operating cost (per seat) of an aircraft while increasing its overall economic performance. This explains why so many of today's airliners come in so many different versions.

But it is not always a simple matter of adding a few more feet to an airplane's length. The A340 and its twin-engine variant, the A330, were given an entirely new wing and many new systems. These costly improvements were necessary in order to enhance the performance and extend the range of the basic A300 design. In the cockpit, the A330 and A340 have more in common with the A319/A320/A321 series than the A300 from which they evolved. In any case, the casual observer will probably see little resemblance between the short-body A310 model and the huge long-range A340.

The same trend applies at the smaller end of the airliner scale, where new versions of the de Havilland Canada Dash 8, the Canadair Regional Jet, and similar aircraft are on the horizon. Regional airlines will be able to add capacity without having to buy an entirely new type of airliner, which would incur considerable additional expense for spare parts and training of crew and maintenance personnel. Commonality adds to both efficiency and economics.

But despite these considerations, manufacturers are considering all-new designs and ever bigger aircraft to carry more passengers at less cost per passenger mile. It is far more likely that we will see an "Ultra-High Capacity Airliner" seating up to 800 people before we see a new supersonic transport. However, both concepts should play a role in the years ahead.

One thing is certain. Airliners will continue to bring people and cultures together, contributing not only to the growth of world trade and commerce, but also to the further development of history's greatest and safest form of mass transportation. I feel comfortable predicting (and you can say you heard it here): the future belongs to aviation!

Appendix: **Airliner specifications and performance**

The rapid growth and development of commercial aviation are depicted in the comparative data presented in the two tables on the next four pages. The table on the first two pages uses American-English measurements while the table on the last two pages uses metric measurements.

Changes in size and performance are for the most part incremental although several dramatic advances represent milestones. The first jetliners, for example, brought about marked increases in speed while the Boeing 747 greatly increased passenger-carrying capacity.

In several instances, data are provided for advanced or derivative versions of basic aircraft, such as the Super Constellation and the stretched DC-8-61.

The senior members of the Boeing family of jetliners—from front to rear the 737, 727, 707, and 747—share a moment together. (Boeing)

Famous Airliners: Specifications (See page 216 for metric measurements)

Ordered by date of first flight	First Flight	Passenger Capacity	Cruising Speed (mph)	Range (miles)	Ceiling (ft)	Length (ft)	Wingspan (ft)	Gross Weight (lb)
Fokker F.VIIa-3m	9/4/25	10	106	550	15,420	47.1	63.4	7,937
Ford Tri-Motor	6/11/26	12–14	122	550	18,500	49.8	77.8	13,000
Lockheed Vega	7/4/27	4–6	150	700	22,000	27.5	41.0	4,270
Boeing Model 80	7/27/28	14–18	125	460	14,000	56.5	80.0	17,500
Junkers Ju 52/3m	10/13/30	14–17	158	545	18,045	62.0	95.9	22,050
Curtiss Condor	1/30/33	15	167	716	23,000	48.6	82.0	17,500
Boeing 247	2/8/33	10	189	840	25,400	51.6	74.0	13,650
Lockheed Model 10	2/23/34	10	182	810	21,650	38.6	55.0	9,750
Douglas DC-2	5/11/34	14–18	196	1,500	23,600	61.9	85.0	18,000
Martin 130 China Clipper	12/30/34	18–46	130	3,200	15,000	90.8	130.0	52,250
Douglas DC-3	12/17/35	21–36	185	1,500	23,200	64.5	95.0	24,000
LZ 129 Hindenburg	3/4/36	72	78	9,000	10,000	803.8	135.2S	485,000
Lockheed Model 14	7/29/37	12	225	1,590	21,500	44.3	65.5	17,500
Boeing 314 Clipper	6/7/38	40–74	184	5,200	19,600	106.0	152.0	84,000
Douglas DC-4E	6/7/38	32–42	219	1,807	22,900	97.6	138.3	65,000
Boeing 307 Stratoliner	12/31/38	33–38	222	1,675	23,800	74.3	107.2	45,000
Lockheed 049 Constellation	1/9/43	48–60	313	3,050	25,000	95.1	123.0	86,250
Douglas DC-6	2/15/46	52	310	2,990	25,000	100.5	117.4	95,200
Martin 202	11/22/46	36–40	286	635	33,000	71.3	93.2	39,900
Convair 240	3/16/47	40	235	690	30,000	74.7	91.7	41,790
Boeing 377 Stratocruiser	7/8/47	89–112	340	2,750	33,000	110.2	141.2	142,500
Vickers Viscount 700	7/16/48	40–46	334	1,750	27,500	81.8	93.7	64,500
de Havilland D.H. 106 Comet 1	7/27/49	36–44	490	1,750	40,000	93.1	115.0	105,000
Avro Canada C102 Jetliner	8/10/49	52	450	1,400	40,000	82.7	98.0	65,000
Bristol Brabazon	9/4/49	80	250	5,500	25,000	177.0	230.0	290,000
Lockheed 1049 Super Constellation	10/13/50	95	327	3,100	25,000	113.6	123.0	150,000
Boeing 707-320	7/15/54*	150–189	605	4,300	42,000	152.8	145.6	333,600
Sud-Aviation Caravelle	5/27/55*	64–80	500	1,056	33,000	105.0	112.5	101,413
Fokker F.27 (Mk 500)	11/24/55*	56	300	1,080	32,600	82.2	95.2	45,000

Douglas DC-7C	12/20/55	110	355	5,640	28,000	112.6	127.5	144,000
Lockheed L-188 Electra	12/6/57	99	405	2,500	27,000	104.7	99.0	116,000
Douglas DC-8	5/30/58	117–179	580	4,300	35,000	150.5	142.4	273,000
Vickers Vanguard	1/20/59	139	425	1,590	30,000	122.9	118.5	146,500
Convair 880	1/27/59	110	615	2,880	41,000	129.3	120.0	193,000
Convair 580	1/19/60	48–56	350	1,700	25,000	81.5	105.3	54,600
Convair 990	1/24/61	121	625	3,800	41,000	139.2	120.0	253,000
de Havilland D.H.121 Trident 1C	1/9/62	103	605	1,150	41,000	114.7	89.8	117,300
Vickers Super VC10	6/29/62*	186	575	4,720	38,000	171.7	146.1	335,000
NAMC YS-11	8/30/62	64	297	860	27,500	86.3	104.9	51,808
Boeing 727-200	2/9/63†	145–189	573	1,670	36,500	153.2	107.9	184,800
BAC One-Eleven	8/20/63	89	540	875	35,000	93.5	88.5	79,000
Douglas DC-9-10	2/25/65	70–90	560	1,310	25,000	104.4	89.4	77,700
de Havilland Canada DHC-6 Twin Otter	5/20/65	18–20	184	920	10,000	49.5	65.0	11,579
Douglas DC-8-61	3/14/66	259	600	3,750	35,000	187.3	142.4	325,000
Boeing 737-100	4/9/67	107	575	2,140	35,000	94.0	93.0	111,000
British Aerospace Jetstream 31	8/18/67	19	300	735	25,000	47.1	52.0	14,550
Boeing 747	2/9/69	350–490	595	5,790	45,000	231.3	195.7	710,000
British Aerospace/Aérospatiale Concorde	3/2/69*	100	1,354	3,970	60,000	205.7	83.8	389,000
McDonnell Douglas DC-10	8/29/70	255–380	584	4,310	42,000	182.2	155.3	440,000
Lockheed L-1011 TriStar	11/17/70	250–400	562	2,677	42,000	178.7	155.3	430,00
VFW 614	7/14/71	44	435	745	25,000	67.6	70.5	44,000
Airbus A300	10/28/72	281–345	582	2,015	40,000	175.9	147.1	347,230
de Havilland Canada Dash 7	3/27/75	50	260	795	21,000	80.5	93.0	44,000
McDonnell Douglas MD-80	10/18/79	139–172	590	1,770	37,000	147.9	107.8	140,000
Boeing 767-200	9/26/81	216	550	5,600	39,000	159.2	156.1	300,000
Boeing 757	2/19/82	186	500	4,590	39,000	155.2	124.5	240,000
Saab 340	1/25/83	30–35	313	1,082	25,000	64.6	70.2	27,275
de Havilland Canada Dash 8	6/20/83	36	345	1,325	25,000	73.0	85.0	34,500
Airbus 320	2/22/87	150–179	556	3,305	37,000	123.0	111.2	162,000
British Aerospace Jetstream 41	9/25/91	29	335	680	26,000	63.2	60.0	19,842
Saab 2000	3/26/92	50	415	1,415	31,000	88.7	81.2	48,500
Boeing 777	6/12/94	375	555	3,970	43,100	209.1	199.9	506,000

* Prototype   † 727-100   § Diameter

Famous Airliners: Metric Specifications (See page 214 for American/English measurements)

Ordered by date of first flight	First Flight	Passenger Capacity	Cruising Speed (km/hr)	Range (km)	Ceiling (m)	Length (m)	Wingspan (m)	Gross Weight (kg)
Fokker F.VIIa-3m	9/4/25	10	171	890	4,700	14.4	19.3	3,600
Ford Tri-Motor	6/11/26	12–14	196	890	5,640	15.2	23.7	5,900
Lockheed Vega	7/4/27	4–6	241	1,130	6,710	8.4	12.5	1,940
Boeing Model 80	7/27/28	14–18	201	740	4,270	17.2	24.4	7,940
Junkers Ju 52/3m	10/13/30	14–17	255	880	5,500	18.9	29.2	10,000
Curtiss Condor	1/30/33	15	269	1,152	7,010	14.8	25.0	7,938
Boeing 247	2/8/33	10	304	1,350	7,740	15.7	22.6	6,190
Lockheed Model 10	2/23/34	10	293	1,300	6,600	11.8	16.8	4,420
Douglas DC-2	5/11/34	14–18	315	2,400	7,190	18.9	25.9	8,170
Martin 130 "China Clipper"	12/30/34	18–46	209	5,150	4,570	27.7	39.6	23,700
Douglas DC-3	12/17/35	21–36	298	2,410	7,070	19.7	29.0	10,890
LZ 129 Hindenburg	3/4/36	72	125	14,500	3,050	245.0	41.2§	220,000
Lockheed Model 14	7/29/37	12	362	2,560	6,560	13.5	20.0	7,940
Boeing 314 Clipper	6/7/38	40–74	296	8,370	5,970	32.3	46.3	38,100
Douglas DC-4E	6/7/38	32–42	352	2,910	6,980	29.7	42.2	29,490
Boeing 307 Stratoliner	12/31/38	33–38	357	2,700	7,250	22.6	32.7	20,410
Lockheed 049 Constellation	1/9/43	48–60	504	4,910	7,620	29.0	37.5	39,110
Douglas DC-6	2/15/46	52	499	4,810	7,620	30.6	35.8	43,180
Martin 202	11/22/46	36–40	460	1,020	10,060	21.7	28.4	18,100
Convair 240	3/16/47	40	378	1,110	9,140	22.8	27.9	18,960
Boeing 377 Stratocruiser	7/8/47	89–112	547	4,430	10,060	33.6	43.0	64,640
Vickers Viscount 700	7/16/48	40–46	538	2,820	8,380	24.9	28.6	29,260
de Havilland D.H. 106 Comet 1	7/27/49	36–44	789	2,820	12,190	28.4	35.1	47,630
Avro Canada C102 Jetliner	8/10/49	52	724	2,250	12,190	25.2	29.9	29,490
Bristol Brabazon	9/4/49	80	402	8,851	7,620	53.9	70.1	131,540
Lockheed 1049 Super Constellation	10/13/50	95	526	4,990	7,620	34.6	37.5	68,100
Boeing 707-320	7/15/54*	150–189	974	6,920	12,800	46.6	44.4	151,320
Sud-Aviation Caravelle	5/27/55*	64–80	805	1,700	10,060	32.0	34.3	46,000
Fokker F.27 (Mk 500)	11/24/55*	56	483	1,740	9,940	25.1	29.0	20,410

Douglas DC-7C	12/20/55	110	571	9,080	8,530	34.3	38.9	65,320
Lockheed L-188 Electra	12/6/57	99	652	4,020	8,230	31.9	30.2	52,620
Douglas DC-8	5/30/58	117–179	933	6,920	10,670	45.9	43.4	123,830
Vickers Vanguard	1/20/59	139	684	2,560	9,145	37.5	36.1	66,451
Convair 880	1/27/59	110	990	4,630	12,500	39.4	36.6	87,540
Convair 580	1/19/60	48–56	563	2,740	7,620	24.8	32.1	24,770
Convair 990	1/24/61	121	1,006	6,115	12,500	42.4	36.6	114,760
de Havilland D.H.121 Trident 1C	1/9/62	103	975	1,850	12,500	34.9	27.4	53,200
Vickers Super VC10	6/29/62*	186	925	7,600	11,580	52.3	44.5	151,950
NAMC YS-11	8/30/62	64	478	1,390	8,380	26.3	32.0	23,500
Boeing 727-200	2/9/63†	145–189	922	2,690	11,130	46.7	32.9	83,820
BAC One-Eleven	8/20/63	89	869	1,410	10,670	28.5	27.0	35,830
Douglas DC-9-10	2/25/65	70–90	901	2,110	7,620	31.8	27.2	35,250
de Havilland Canada DHC-6 Twin Otter	5/20/65	18–20	296	1,480	3,050	15.1	19.8	5,250
Douglas DC-8-61	3/14/66	259	966	6,040	10,670	57.1	43.4	147,420
Boeing 737-100	4/9/67	107	925	3,440	10,670	28.6	28.3	50,350
British Aerospace Jetstream 31	8/18/67	19	482	1,185	7,620	14.4	15.8	6,600
Boeing 747	2/9/69	350–490	958	9,320	13,720	70.5	59.6	322,050
British Aerospace/Aérospatiale Concorde	3/2/69*	100	2,179	6,390	18,290	62.7	25.5	176,450
McDonnell Douglas DC-10	8/29/70	255–380	940	6,940	12,800	55.5	47.3	199,580
Lockheed L-1011 TriStar	11/17/70	250–400	904	4,310	12,800	54.5	47.3	195,050
VFW 614	7/14/71	44	700	1,200	7,620	20.6	21.5	19,950
Airbus A300	10/28/72	281–345	937	3,240	12,190	53.6	44.8	157,500
de Havilland Canada Dash 7	3/27/75	50	420	1,280	6,400	24.5	28.3	19,958
McDonnell Douglas MD-80	10/18/79	139–172	950	2,850	11,280	45.1	32.9	63,500
Boeing 767-200	9/26/81	216	885	9,010	11,890	48.5	47.6	136,078
Boeing 757	2/19/82	186	805	7,385	11,890	47.3	38.0	108,864
Saab 340	1/25/83	30–35	504	1,740	7,620	19.7	21.4	12,370
de Havilland Canada Dash 8	6/20/83	36	555	2,130	7,620	22.2	25.9	15,650
Airbus 320	2/22/87	150–179	895	5,320	11,280	37.5	33.9	73,500
British Aerospace Jetstream 41	9/25/91	29	541	1,095	7,925	19.2	18.3	9,000
Saab 2000	3/26/92	50	668	2,280	9,450	27.0	24.7	22,000
Boeing 777	6/12/94	375	893	6,390	13,137	63.7	60.9	229,520

* Prototype   † 727-100   § Diameter

Bibliography

Many of the sources listed here are out of print, and some were never available to the public since they were published by manufacturers as marketing aids. Used book stores, the classified sections of aviation magazines, and airliner conventions are good places to find out-of-print books and secondhand aviation journals.

The many fine aviation museums around the world provide close-up looks at historic aircraft. Curators are usually quite willing to help researchers, while shop managers can help find books that appeal to individual interests. The more you find out about aviation history, the more you will want to learn!

Books

Berk, William and Frank. *Guide to Airport Airplanes*. Plymouth, Michigan: Plymouth Press, 2nd edition, 1996.

Birtles, Philip J. *de Havilland Comet*. Shepperton, Surrey: Ian Allen, Ltd., 1990.

Birtles, Philip, and Allen Burney. *Concorde*. Shepperton, Surrey: Ian Allen, Ltd., 1986.

Boeing. *Pedigree of Champions*. Seattle: The Boeing Company, 1985.

British Aircraft Corporation. *Concorde Technical Description*. London: British Aircraft Corporation, 1969.

————. *Concorde: The Competitive Edge*. London: British Aircraft Corporation, 1973.

Cohen, Stan. *Wings to the Orient*. Missoula, Montana: Pictorial Histories Publishing Company, 1985.

Douglas Aircraft Company. *The DC-8 Story*. Long Beach: McDonnell Douglas Corporation, 1972.

————. *DC-10 Design Features*. Long Beach: McDonnell Douglas Corporation, 1981.

————. *The DC-9 Handbook*. Long Beach: McDonnell Douglas Corporation, 1983.

————. *McDonnell Douglas Commercial Family: DC-1 through MD-80*. Long Beach: McDonnell Douglas Corporation, 1985.

Drury, George H. *The Train-Watcher's Guide to North American Railroads*. Waukesha, Wisconsin: Kalmbach Publishing Company, 1992.

Floyd, Jim. *The Avro Canada C102 Jetliner*. Erin, Ontario: The Boston Mills Press, 1986.

Fokker, Anthony H.G., and Bruce Gould. *Flying Dutchman*. Henry Holt & Company, 1931. Reprint. New York: Arno Press, 1972.

Green, William, Gordon Swanborough, and John Mowinski. *Modern Commercial Aircraft*. London: Salamander Books, 1987.

Hedley, Martin. *Vickers VC10*. Shepperton, Surrey: Ian Allen, Ltd., 1982.

Hegener, Henri. *Fokker: The Man and the Aircraft*. Letchworth, Hertfordshire: Harleyford Publications, 1961.

Hotson, Fred W. *The de Havilland Canada Story*. Toronto: CANAV Books, 1983.

Ingells, Douglas J. *The Plane that Changed the World: A Biography of the DC-3*. Fallbrook, California: Aero Publishers, Inc., 1966.

————. *Tin Goose*. Fallbrook, California: Aero Publishers, Inc., 1968.

————. *747: Story of the Boeing Super Jet*. Fallbrook, California: Aero Publishers, Inc., 1970.

————. *L-1011 TriStar and the Lockheed Story*. Fallbrook, California: Aero Publishers, Inc., 1973.

————. *The McDonnell Douglas Story*. Fallbrook, California: Aero Publishers, Inc., 1979.

Munson, Kenneth. *Airliners from 1919 to the Present Day*. Revised ed. New York: Exeter Books, 1983.

Olson, Bjorn. *The Saab-Scania Story*. Stockholm: Streiffert & Company, 1987.

Postma, Thijs. *Fokker: Aircraft Builders to the World*. London: Jane's Publishing Company Ltd., 1980.

Sweetman, William. *A History of Passenger Aircraft*. London: Hamlyn Publishing Group, Ltd., 1979.

Taylor, Frank J. *High Horizons*. New York: McGraw-Hill Book Company, Inc., 1964.

Taylor, John W.R., and Kenneth Munson. *History of Aviation*. New York: Crown Publishers, Inc., 1972.

Taylor, John W.R., ed. *Jane's All the World's Aircraft* (1962-63). London: Jane's Publishing Company Ltd., 1962.

————. *Jane's All the World's Aircraft* (1969-70). London: Jane's Publishing Company Ltd., 1969.

Wall, Robert. *Airliners*. Secaucus, New Jersey: Chartwell Books, 1980.

————. *Ocean Liners*. Secaucus, New Jersey: Chartwell Books, 1977.

Warwick, Ronald W., and William H. Flayhart III. *QE2*. New York: W.W. Norton & Company, 1985.

Wood, Derek. *Project Cancelled*. London: Jane's Publishing Company Ltd., 1975.

Young, David, and Neal Callahan. *Fill the Heavens with Commerce*. Chicago: Chicago Review Press, 1981.

Periodicals

Aeroplane

Aircraft Engineering

Air Enthusiast

Air International

Airliners

Airways

Aviation Week & Space Technology

Flight International

Flying Review

Interavia

The Putnam Aeronautical Review

Acknowledgments

Writing a history usually requires the assistance and support of a number of people who are willing to provide assorted information and photographs. *Famous Airliners* is no exception, and the author is indebted to those who have so generously given both material help and sound advice.

Famous Airliners owes its origins to a series of monthly articles written for Midway Airlines' in-flight magazine several years ago. I am indebted to *Midway* editor, Terri Wallo, for her early support, and also to my publishers at Plymouth Press for all of their work in producing this book.

The author's personal aviation reference library, from which most of the information used in this book was drawn, has been assembled over the past quarter century with the help of many colleagues and associates, in particular: Jeffrey H. Erickson, former president of Trans World Airlines, Midway Airlines, and Reno Air; Stuart Matthews, Chairman of the Flight Safety Foundation and former chairman of Fokker Aircraft USA; Thomas L. Tucker, former Area Marketing Director for Douglas Aircraft Company; Hartmut F. Klein, Manager of Strategy for Daimler Benz Aerospace Airbus GmbH; Olof Koppenberg, Regional Sales Director for Airbus Industrie; Leroy Simpson, former Vice President of Sales Engineering for Fokker Aircraft USA and a former flight engineer on board Pan American's Boeing 314 Clippers (as well as my former boss).

In addition, technical information, personal interviews, and much support has come from the following individuals: Peter Alting, Thomas Appleton, Dr. George Bloomfield, Jim Burk, Robert W. Bradford, Christopher Cooper-Slipper, Dick and Paula Eastman, Colin Fisher, Dr. Michael A. Fopp, Larry Freudinger, Harry S. Gann, Josef Grendel, Asa Holm, Harry Holmes, Michael Jolley, Steven J. Khachaturian, Otto M. Kohler, Fred Matthews, Steve McNeilly, William J. O'Donnell, Mario Pesando, Jon Proctor, Donald Rogers, Anne Rutledge, Eric Schulzinger, Victor Seely, Ronald Sherman, Allan Smolinski, R. Dixon Speas, Paul Spitzer, Gerard van Putten, Nicholas Veronico, John Wegg, and James Woolsey…to name a few!

A very special "Thank you" goes to my parents, Frank and Lorraine Mellberg, who early in my life spawned my interest in both aviation and writing. Their love and guidance helped a lot. My brother, John Mellberg, provided both his expertise and the photographs for the chapter on the airship *Hindenburg*.

Last, but certainly not least, I want to thank my hero and mentor, James C. Floyd, for writing the foreword to *Famous Airliners*. Jim and his wife, Irene, have extended their friendship and hospitality during my many visits to Canada. And Jim's very remarkable aviation career, as well as his own literary works, provided much of the inspiration for *Famous Airliners*. It has been my privilege to know him.

Thanks also to the following organizations for providing the many splendid photographs which grace the pages of **Famous Airliners**: Airbus Industrie, Air Canada, Air France, American Airlines, BOAC, Bombardier Regional Aircraft, Braniff Airways, British Aerospace, British Airways, Boeing, Continental Airlines, de Havilland Canada, Delta Air Lines, Eastern Airlines, Fairchild-Hiller, Fokker Aircraft, Frontier Airlines, General Dynamics, Lockheed Aircraft, Lufthansa German Airlines, McDonnell Douglas, Midway Airlines, the Museum of Flight (Seattle), the National Aviation Museum (Ottawa), North Central Airlines, Northwest Airlines, Ozark Air Lines, Pan American Airways, Piedmont Airlines, the Royal Canadian Mounted Police, the Royal Air Force, SAAB, Scandanavian Airlines System, United Airlines, and the White House.

Index

About the Author

Bill Mellberg is a well-known aerospace writer and historian. His articles in aerospace publications have reached audiences around the globe. Bill was graduated from the University of Illinois at Urbana-Champaign in 1975 and has worked for Fokker Aircraft U.S.A. and for Ozark Air Lines in marketing and public relations. He is also a nationally recognized political satirist and speaker who has starred in several television specials for PBS. A native of Chicago, he currently resides near O'Hare Field—where you'll find him looking up whenever an airliner passes over.

abc Airline Series!

Each book in this series spotlights one of the world's major airlines. With words and pictures—many in color—the reader is transported from the humble origins of each of the airlines through its evolution into a large and important carrier. *Included for each carrier:* information on current operations, fleet configurations, route systems, and more.

Series specs: 7 1/4" by 4 3/4", 96 pages, soft cover

abc Northwest Airlines
by Geoff Jones
ISBN 1-882663-28-4
Item #PP-NA **$12.95**

abc United Airlines
by Simon Forty
ISBN 1-882663-20-9
Item #PP-UA **$12.95**

abc American Airlines
by Simon Forty
ISBN 1-882663-21-7
Item #PP-AA **$12.95**

abc Delta Airlines
by Geoff Jones
ISBN 1-882663-29-2
Item #PP-DA **$12.95**

abc British Airways
by Leo Marriott
ISBN 1-882663-39-X
Item #PP-BA **$12.95**

abc US Airways
by Leo Marriott
ISBN 1-882663-27-6
Item #PP-US **$12.95**

abc Cargo Airlines
by Alan J. Wright
ISBN 1-882663-45-4
Item #PP-CO **$12.95**

Airliner Note Cards

Featuring beautiful color paintings by Richard King

We commissioned our favorite aviation artist to create six new airliner paintings especially for these note card sets. Modern airliners make up one set, while beloved vintage airliners are depicted in the other. Cards are of heavy stock, measure 5 by 6 5/8 inches folded, and are packed in attractive, sturdy boxes. *Each set includes 9 note cards and 9 envelopes, 3 each of 3 paintings.*

Jetliners

Vintage Airliners

Modern Jetliners set *includes Boeing 747, Airbus A300, McDonnell Douglas DC-9*
ISBN 1-882663-18-7
PP-JET **$9.95**

Vintage Airliners set *includes Douglas DC-3, Ford Trimotor, China Clipper*
ISBN 1-882663-19-5
PP-VINT **$9.95**

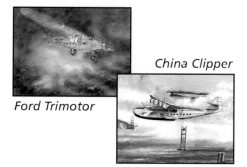

China Clipper

Ford Trimotor

McDonnell Douglas DC-9

Airbus A300

Boeing Airliners
747/757/767 in Color
by Alan J. Wright & Robbie Shaw

Boeing is a name that is synonymous with the giant jetliners which traverse the world's airways. The company's Boeing 747, with its humped forward fuselage, has become an icon of the jet age. This book covers the continuously updated 747; and its modern siblings, the narrow-bodied 757 and wide-bodied 767. Includes over 100 color pictures.

6 3/4" by 9 1/4", 128 pages, soft cover, ISBN 1-882663-24-1
Item #PP-BAL **$24.95**

More aircraft recognition guides!

For light aircraft, vintage aircraft, combat aircraft...

Light Aircraft Recognition
3rd edition
by Peter March

This guide to recognition gives all the information that spotters will need to identify the small prop planes and helicopters commonly seen on airport runways...and in local skies. *Includes such well known craft as the Piper Cherokee, Piper Super Cub, Aeronca Champion, and the Cessna 150 and 180.*

4 1/2" by 7", 108 pages, soft cover
ISBN 1-882663-15-2
Item #PP-LAR3 .... $11.95

Classic & Warbird Recognition
by Peter March

A great guide to take to airshows and air museums, or just to browse at home. This book covers vintage aircraft—both civilian and military—which are kept in flying condition by individuals and museums around the world. Each entry offers details of the history and performance capabilities of these beloved planes. *Includes over 100 photos of the classic birds in flight.*

4 1/5" by 7", 96 pages, soft cover
ISBN 0-7110-2423-5
Item #IA-CLWB $12.95

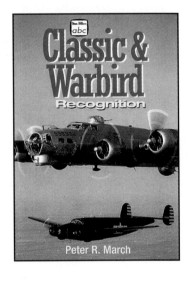

Combat Aircraft Recognition 3rd edition
by Peter March

The definitive guide to the recognition of military aircraft flown around the world by nations great and small. They're all here, from the McDonnell Douglas F-15 to the Boeing B-52 to the MiG-29 and European Tornado fighters, and more. *Includes choppers as well as fixed wing craft.*

4 1/2" by 7", 108 pages, soft cover
ISBN 1-882663-26-8
Item #PP-CAR3 .... $14.95

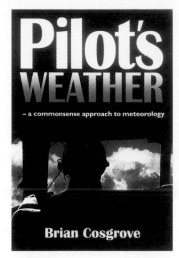

Pilot's Weather
A Commonsense Approach to Meteorology
by Brian Cosgrove

This remarkable and beautiful new book enters uncharted territory in explaining the vitally important pilot skill of understanding atmospheric peturbations. Rather than "teaching" with dreary old black and white drawings of isobars and fronts and endless graphs and reams of figures, **Pilot's Weather** provides full-color photos and clear explanations of what fliers actually see and experience. Printed on high quality gloss paper which shows off to advantage its many beautiful illustrations and photos, **Pilot's Weather** excels at making weather comprehensible to the non-meteorologist. This book is for readers who are interested in flying aircraft, ultralights, gliders, or kites—or whose interest is the weather itself.

About the author: *Brian Cosgrove is an award-winning author and microlight enthusiast whose previous books are The Microlight Pilot's Handbook and The World of Weather.*

Includes 153 full-color photos and 114 line drawings...

9 1/4" by 6 1/4", 192 pages, hard cover, ISBN 1-882663-41-1
Item # PP-PW **$34.95**

Airline Nostalgia
Classic Aircraft in Color
by Adrian Balch

With remarkable full-color pictures, this book brings to life aircraft whose origin is a distant era. Readers who love airliners will enjoy the classic lines of a "Connnie" (Lockheed Constellation) as she swoops low onto the runway or of the workhorse Douglas DC-3 at rest on the tarmac. **Airline Nostalgia** ranges chronologically from airliners originating in the 1930s—such as the DC-3—and continues up to the early jetliners, such as the de Havilland Comet and Boeing 707. It also includes older versions of such current models as the Boeing 727 and 747. *Many photos show these veteran airliners in recent action.*

About the author: *Adrian Balm is an internationally known writer, photographer, and airliner enthusiast. He has carefully chosen the photos for this book from his collection over 100,000 color slides.*

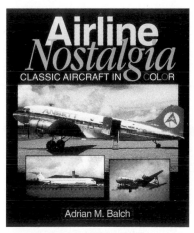

Includes 150 full-color photos...

10 1/2" by 9", 112 pages, soft cover, .
ISBN 1-882663-42-X
Item # PP-AN **$29.95**

Fly these desktop Famous Airliners!

For those who command the very best, or wish they did, we bring you the ultimate in display models. All are featured in **Famous Airliners***; all are hand fashioned with rich mahogany, sleek resin, or high quality plastic.*

If you don't see it, ask for it...hundreds of models available.

TWA Super Connie
Wood...1:100 scale...$87.95

Description	W = wood R= resin P= plastic	Material	Scale	Price
Vintage Airliners				
DC-3 *American, Delta, Eastern or TWA*		W	1:72	$104.95
DC-6B, DC-6C or DC-7B *American*		W	1:100	96.95
DC-8 *TWA*		W	1:72	89.95
DC-8-71 *United*		W	1:100	119.95
Boeing B-247 *United*		W	1:48	112.95
Boeing B-314 Clipper flying boat *Pan Am*		W	1:100	96.95
Boeing 377 Stratocruiser *United or American*		W	1:100	97.95
Boeing 707-320 *American, Pan Am or TWA*		W	1:100	112.95
Lockheed 1049 Constellation *Eastern or TWA*		W	1:100	96.95
Martin M-130 China Clipper flying boat *Pan Am*		P	1:72	127.95
Martin 404 *TWA*		W	1:72	97.95
Modern Airliners				
Airbus A320 *Northwest*		R	1:100	$104.95
Bae Jetstream 31 *American Eagle*		W	1:48	97.95
Boeing 727-200 *American, Northwest, Pan Am or TWA*		R	1:100	104.95
Boeing 737-300 *USAir*		R	1:100	112.95
Boeing 747 *NASA with piggyback Space Shuttle*		P	1:200	104.95
Boeing 747-200 *Japan Air, Northwest, Pan Am, TWA or United*		P	1:200	81.95
Boeing 747-400 *Northwest or United*		P	1:200	89.95
Boeing 757-200 *American*		R	1:100	127.95
Boeing 767-300 *American*		R	1:100	142.95
Boeing 777 *United*		R	1:200	96.95
Concorde *Air France or British Airways*		R	1:100	127.95
DC-10 *United Cargo*		P	1:200	58.95
DC-10-30 *American*		P	1:200	58.95
L-1011 TriStar *TWA*		W	1:100	142.95
MD-11 *American or Delta*		R	1:164	112.95
MD-80 *American, Delta, Northwest or TWA*		R	1:100	104.95
MD-90 *Delta*		R	1:100	112.95
Saab 240 *American Eagle*		W	1:48	97.95

Jetliner pilot answers the questions that flying travelers are most curious about...

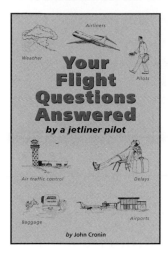

Jetliner pilot John Cronin enjoys talking with his passengers about their flying experiences. Over his years of piloting airliners he has collected the questions which flying travelers most frequently ask. Now he presents his answers this new book. Pilot Cronin explains:

- **how airliners fly and navigate**
- **airports—how they work**
- **air traffic control**
- **weather and its effects on airliners**
- **what causes delays**

and many other issues related to flying.

Some of the questions answered by pilot Cronin:

✈ *How does air traffic control provide guidance to pilots?*

✈ *As the airliner I'm flying in prepares to land, the sound of the engines is constantly changing. Why?*

✈ *What is the little red and white shack I see by the runway?*

✈ *Sometimes when I'm flying, my ears bother me. What can I do to make them feel better?*

✈ *How does a person become a pilot?*   ✈ *How does a jet engine work?*

✈ *What makes an airliner fly?*   ✈ *How is my luggage processed?*

Raves for *Your Flight Questions Answered*:

"…quickly became a favorite source among the public relations people in my office…gives easy-to-understand answers to complex aviation questions. Best of all, it's a fun read." Ray Scippa, **Continental Airlines**

"Offers preventative advice to those of us who have watched our planes take off without us, lost our luggage, or spent hours in a 'connecting' airport with no connection in sight…" **Consumer's Digest**

"*Your Flight Questions Answered* will be of interest to both white-knuckle fliers and those who clamor for the window seat." John Sotham, *Air & Space* Smithsonian magazine

"Covers many of the questions I'm frequently asked, and a few that I've wanted to ask myself. It would be nice to have copies in airline seat pockets." James P. Woolsey, Senior Editor, *Air Transport World*

"It's like having a friend in the aviation industry to provide you with an insider's point of view." Lane Brafford, **US Airways**

Your Flight Questions Answered

5 1/2 by 8 1/2 inches, 112 pages, ISBN 1-882663-23-3
Item #PP-YFQ $9.95

We love airliners! And we have plenty of great books to help you learn about them...

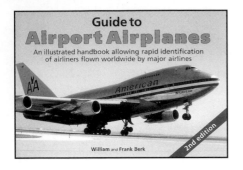

Guide to Airport Airplanes
by William *and* Frank Berk

Includes color photos and 3-view silhouettes of commonly observed airliners

Facilitating identification of airliners with its simple-to-use, systematic approach, the *Guide* features the 66 most commonly observed airliners, all pictured in color photographs while in flight or at interesting airport locales. Capabilities, as well as country of origin and date of first flight are included, making the *Guide* an excellent basic reference as well as an indispensable airport companion.

The experts agree: if you're going to have one airliner book with you at the airport, this is the one...

"A great aid in aircraft identification." Hemispheres (United Airline's in-flight magazine)

"A handy guide that can be taken along on trips for quick identification." Toronto Star

"A marvelous reference book..." Robert W. Bradford, retired Director, National Aviation Museum, Canada

"This updated all-color second edition is a handy source of information for airliner photographers and spotters... a must when shooting (photographs of) airliners." Airliners magazine

"Makes identification of airliners easy...a great gift." American Aviation Historical Society

7" by 5", 168 pages, soft cover, ISBN 1-882663-10-1
Item #PP-GAP2 .... **$14.95**

The Airport Airplane Coloring Book
by Richard King

Travelers and airliner buffs can bring the romance of the airport home or have their airport experience enhanced by *The Airport Airplane Coloring Book*. It includes airliners often observed at major airports, such as the Boeing 727, 737, and 747; the McDonnell-Douglas DC-9 and DC-10; and the Airbus A300.

"Hours of fun coloring...the perfect gift for an aviation minded youngster." Airliners magazine

8 1/2" by 11", 44 pages, soft cover, ISBN 1-882663-05-5
Item #PP-AACC **$5.95**